'This volume is an exciting guide for helping children to find health and happiness. Sexuality education is not an easy topic; however, the authors have managed to combine evidence, experience and fun. The study is a major contribution to the understanding of children, adults and the world.'

– Prof. Gunta Lazdane, former regional adviser,
sexual and reproductive health, WHO/Europe

'It is really refreshing to read a book about relationships that deals with sexuality in such a frank, honest and helpful way. As well as explaining developmental expectations, it also gives ideas for answering those tricky questions that children always seem to ask when you least expect it!'

– Laura King, primary school teacher and mum of three

'As a parent and psychotherapist, I found this book a refreshing, ease-inducing guide to educating children about their bodies, sex and beyond. Many can feel overwhelmed or ill-equipped to speak to their children about these matters. This book offers hope and centralizes the parent–child bond as the conduit to give children a realistic and positive relationship with their bodies, senses and eventual sexuality. Highly recommend it.'

– Erica Esmail-Rath, MFT psychotherapist
practising in San Francisco, California

'This book transformed my concept of parental responsibility for sex education from the conventional approach of a single, well-timed presentation (aka "The Talk") into an appreciation of sexuality as an aspect of child development to be interwoven into my day-to-day relationships with my children. I wish I had this book a decade ago when I began my motherhood journey. It would make an amazing baby shower gift for any parent-to-be.'

– Amanda Bealer, US,
mother of Carson (age 8) and Chase (age 11)

'Well written, easy-to-read and very insightful. Gives an excellent overview of this important subject and practical, age-appropriate tips on how to educate children of all ages on sexuality and relationships. This will hopefully allow the next generation to grow up without the embarrassment, misconceptions and prejudices of generations before. The world has changed and it's time for education around this subject to change as well.'

– Louise Speggiorin, health visitor, UK

'Can I Have Babies Too? takes us parents by the hand so we can become self-assured sex and relationships educators to our children. That's never straightforward – but this book is. With its clear and helpful Dutch approach, it schools us all in how and why to talk openly, starting now…'

– Leah Jewett, Director, Outspoken Sex Ed

'This book is a lifeline for any parent, carer or educator, packed with honest, practical advice for each stage of childhood. The authors draw on years of experience working with children, as well as research in health and psychology, to offer a positive vision for how to talk to children about bodies, relationships and sexuality.'

– Joanna Herat, UN Health and Education specialist, and parent

'I found this book insightful by wrapping the wider subject of sexuality education around the traditionally thorny topic of sex education. It helps and encourages children to understand themselves before attempting to understand others and their own personal interactions. Raises important topics with an interesting boldness, highlighting the probable need to start earlier than many parents, including myself, appreciated.'

– Nick Reynolds, father of a 9-year-old boy

'This book provides a very sensitive, reflective way to enable parents and people around young children to talk about sexuality, offering tools and answering questions frequently considered taboo. It embodies the idea of holistic sexuality and empowerment, and implements an age-appropriate approach to comprehensive sexuality education.'

– Johanna Marquardt, Project Officer for the WHO Collaboration Centre/BZgA for sexual and reproductive health

'I dream of a world in which every child can be taught about relationships and sexuality in the caring, honest, dignified, non-judgemental and truly child-centered manner this book models for parents and teachers. The authors' approach is patient and generous, and their message, while it may still seem revolutionary in countries such as the United States, is sensible, practical and proven: young people of all ages have the right to comprehensive knowledge about bodies, friendship and love. When this right is respected, children are empowered to make lifelong, good choices, allowing them to enjoy, respect and safeguard their hearts, minds and bodies – as well as those belonging to others.

This small book has the power to transform the next generation of children and to empower parents and educators to give young people the self-esteem, confidence, respect and empathy it takes to build healthy, equal and fulfilling relationships. I will be emphatically recommending this book to all of the parents and educators I work with.

In abundant sample scripts, this book models how it sounds to impart true autonomy even to very young children. Importantly, too, the authors present a broad range of normal childhood "sexual" behaviours, delivering the much-needed message that we need not get so bent out of shape about the sometimes eyebrow-raising ways in which children learn and play.'

– Bonnie J. Rough, author of Beyond Birds and Bees:
Bringing Home a New Message to
Our Kids about Sex, Love, and Equality

Can I Have Babies Too?

of related interest

Talking Consent
16 Workshops on Relationship and Sex Education
for Schools and Other Youth Settings
Thalia Wallis and Pete Wallis
ISBN 978 1 78775 081 4
eISBN 978 1 78775 082 1

Ask First, Monkey!
A Playful Introduction to Consent and Boundaries
Juliet Clare Bell
Illustrated by Abigail Tompkins
ISBN 978 1 78775 410 2
eISBN 978 1 78775 411 9

Gender Equality in Primary Schools
A Guide for Teachers
Helen Griffin
ISBN 978 1 78592 340 1
eISBN 978 1 78450 661 2

The Every Body Book
The LGBTQ+ Inclusive Guide for Kids about
Sex, Gender, Bodies, and Families
Rachel E. Simon, LCSW
Illustrated by Noah Grigni
ISBN 978 1 78775 173 6
eISBN 978 1 78775 174 3

Can I Have Babies Too?

Sexuality and Relationships Education for Children from Infancy up to Age 11

Sanderijn van der Doef,
Clare Bennett and Arris Lueks

Jessica Kingsley Publishers
London and Philadelphia

First published in Great Britain in 2021 by Jessica Kingsley Publishers
An Hachette Company

1

Copyright © Sanderijn van der Doef, Clare Bennett and Arris Lueks 2021
Illustration copyright © Liese Stuer 2021
Illustration copyright © Sensoa Flag System, Garant Publishers 2018

Front cover image source: Shutterstock®.

A CIP catalogue record for this title is available from the
British Library and the Library of Congress

ISBN 978 1 78775 500 0
eISBN 978 1 78775 501 7

Printed and bound in Great Britain by CPI Group

Jessica Kingsley Publishers' policy is to use papers that are natural,
renewable and recyclable products and made from wood grown in
sustainable forests. The logging and manufacturing processes are expected
to conform to the environmental regulations of the country of origin.

Jessica Kingsley Publishers
Carmelite House
50 Victoria Embankment
London EC4Y 0DZ

www.jkp.com

To our mothers who taught us how to become mothers
and to our children for teaching us how to be mothers.

Voor onze moeders die ons geleerd hebben moeder te worden
en voor onze kinderen die ons geleerd hebben moeder te zijn.

Contents

Acknowledgements   13

Preface   15

Introduction   18

1. Being in Touch with Your Child   25

2. Challenges and Opportunities in Discussing
    Sexuality with Children   38

3. Communicating with Children about Sexuality   52

4. Social and Sexual Development in Children   66

5. Supporting Children's Development and Learning in
    Relationships and Sexuality: Birth to Three Years   82

6. Supporting Children's Development and Learning in
    Relationships and Sexuality: Four to Six Years   102

7. Supporting Children's Development and Learning in
    Relationships and Sexuality: Seven to Nine Years   131

8. Supporting Children's Development and Learning in
    Relationships and Sexuality: Ten to Eleven Years   159

9. 'Is this Okay?'   188

10. What Next?   206

    Resources   212

    References   217

Acknowledgements

Writing a book like this is never easy. Although much of the content was already there, in our own research, training materials and through the knowledge we acquire every day in our professional lives, we still needed help from other experts. We listened to parents, carers and grandparents; we asked teachers and other educators questions; we read books and articles and we even consulted our own children! Many people deserve special thanks for supporting us in helping to develop the book and in shaping what we have written. Without their support, this book wouldn't be the comprehensive resource it has become.

Several expert readers closely read and commented on the manuscript; their comments have contributed tremendously to enhancing the quality of the book and for this we sincerely thank them. Susie Jolly of the Institute of Development Studies and an independent consultant, researcher and facilitator, thank you so much for your valuable comments and ideas, especially about gender and gender equality. Thank you too to Sensoa, and especially Erika Frans, for allowing and helping us to describe the Sensoa Flag System. Sincere thanks must also be given to the Winston Churchill Memorial Trust and Cardiff University's Erasmus+ Organisational Mobility for funding the original projects from which this book evolved. Thanks too to Peter Oates of Lantern Press for helping us find a publisher for this book and to James Cherry for supporting us in securing a contract for publication.

Finally, we wish to extend our gratitude to the parents, carers, teachers and kindergarten staff in the UK, US, Canada and Australia who were so generous in telling us what topics they wanted us to address in this book. We hope we have done you proud!

Preface

How many times as a parent or carer have you thought: *Now's the time to talk with my child about the birds and the bees?* And how many times have you stopped just before starting 'the talk' because it was too embarrassing or difficult? Likewise, if you're a teacher and it's your job to 'do' relationships and sexuality education, do you feel some trepidation?

Finding the right words, the correct expressions, the right moment and coping with the response when you start your first sentence: 'Listen, it's time to talk about how babies are made' are enough to put many adults off talking about relationships and sexuality with a child. Not to mention how the opening sentence is likely to make the child feel if this is a completely new topic for them. In this book, we introduce you to an alternative, less stressful and more effective approach to relationships and sexuality education for young children – one which considers this aspect of children's learning as an integral part of their day-to-day education rather than something separate, requiring a single, isolated 'talk'.

Throughout this book, we draw on our extensive collective professional experience, which includes teaching children, their carers and professionals about relationships and sexuality education as well as conducting research in the field. Sanderijn van der Doef is a psychologist and sexologist, a counsellor, a trainer and an author. She has written many books about relationships and sexuality education for children and parents, which have sold internationally. She travels all over the world to give training, workshops and presentations on the importance of relationships and sexuality education for children and adolescents. Clare Bennett is a senior lecturer at Cardiff University and a nurse with a background in sexual health. Her doctorate was about parent-child sexuality communication in the UK and she subsequently explored this theme further in the Netherlands. Clare has published, taught and presented in this field internationally. Arris Lueks works at HAN University of Applied Sciences in the Netherlands, where she has taught thousands of trainee teachers how to introduce relationships and sexuality education into the primary school curriculum. Arris is experienced in teaching the Flag System, developed by Erika Frans from Sensoa, a Belgian expertise centre for sexual reproductive health, and has given several workshops in the UK regarding relationships and sexuality education.

Importantly though, in addition to drawing on our professional expertise throughout this book, we also draw on our personal experiences of parenthood and dealing with children's tricky questions that always seem to be posed very loudly in the most inappropriate environments! We also draw on the relevant research evidence in the field.

We understand that children's relationships and sexuality education can be contentious and highly sensitive. What we hope to offer you here is an evidence-based, practical approach to teaching children about this important aspect of development. In writing the book, the three of us have discovered that we have slightly different perspectives and we expect that our readers will all have different perspectives too. We do not intend to lecture or preach but instead we hope to inspire confidence in you to introduce relationships and sexuality to children early, in a way that works for you and the children you care for. Taking care of children, showing them affection, teaching them how to interact and show empathy, explaining about equality and demonstrating positive role modelling are important parts of relationships and sexuality education. We understand that sometimes 'a talk' is necessary but consciously integrating relationships and sexuality education into your daily interactions with children might make such 'talks' easier, more spontaneous and more effective.

We sincerely hope that our book will be helpful to you in facilitating the long and gradual process of relationships and sexuality education. Don't wait to have 'the talk' and don't stop after one 'talk'; instead, use all the opportunities that everyday life presents, along with some of the tips we give you in this book, to prompt communication about relationships and sexuality.

With our very best wishes,
Sanderijn, Clare and Arris

Introduction

Who is this book for?

When we decided to write this book, we went out and spoke to parents, grandparents, foster parents, teachers, kindergarten staff, social workers, nurses and many others. We also trawled through and analysed relevant parenting websites from around the world. We wanted to know what the challenges were for parents, carers and professionals when teaching young children about relationships and sexuality. We weren't expecting such a positive response! The people we spoke to had long lists of questions and the overwhelming message was that adults need help in how to have these conversations and, in particular, they want advice on how to answer tricky questions. Here are some of the examples they gave:

'My six-year-old asked me: "Can two boys make a baby?" What should I say?'

'My ten-year-old asked me: "If I get my period when I'm

away on holiday, can I just hold it in like a wee?" To be honest, as a dad I'm not sure!'

Other questions were more concerned with how to respond to children's behaviours, for example:

'What should I do when a child in my class touches their genitals at story time?'

'How should I react when my child asks to play "doctors" with a friend?'

Are these kinds of questions familiar to you? Could you do with some help? If so, this book is for you! However, if these kinds of questions haven't (yet) emerged for you, this book is for you too, as a lack of opportunities for these kinds of conversations offers a different type of challenge, as we'll discuss later.

We have written this book for parents, grandparents, foster parents, carers, teachers, pre-school staff, healthcare professionals, psychologists, pedagogists and anyone else who cares for or works with young children. Although we sometimes directly address parents, this doesn't mean other professional and non-professional carers should feel ignored, it is just that certain aspects of relationships and sexuality education are more likely to occur in the private space of the home.

When we write about families in this book, we realize that families exist in many different forms. Children may grow up with a father and mother or with two parents of the same sex or with one parent. Children may also grow up in extended families, in foster families or with step-parents. There are also children who, for a variety of reasons, grow up in institutions.

Regardless of the kind of home a child grows up in, every child has the right to support, safety and guidance. Every child also has the right to accurate, age- and developmentally appropriate information to guide them in their search for answers to their questions. We hope that this book helps you to address these particular children's rights, regardless of the shape of their family.

Just a note about culture; we are an international team of authors with international experience and we know that discussing relationships and sexuality with children can be a challenge in some cultures, sometimes even a taboo. This book clearly has a European slant, with two of the three authors coming from the Netherlands where relationships and sexuality education is considered normal and useful even for very young children. These ideas about relationships and sexuality education might sometimes be different, challenging or maybe even provocative. With Clare's help (coming from the UK and aware of different views on this topic), we have made some adaptations to suit the UK, US, Canadian and Australian context, but most of our Dutch and European ideas are still there.

As you read this book, you will find, in certain sections, that we have our own particular values and opinions on specific topics. Although we give you objective, evidence-based information, we cannot and do not want to be totally neutral. However, we do not intend to impose our values on you. Instead, we want to provide you with guidance and information based on research that shows what methods of relationships and sexuality education are effective and helpful for children.

What is this book about?

This book is about helping young children to learn about relationships and sexuality. When we talk about 'sexuality' we are not just talking about sex. Sexuality is a broad term that encompasses how we feel about our bodies, identity, sexual feelings and expression, gender, reproduction, love, closeness, personal values and relationships. When we discuss 'sexuality education', we need to be clear from the outset that we are *not* talking about teaching children how to have sex. Nor are we promoting the idea that being in a relationship or having sex is vital to people's happiness. Sexuality education is about guiding children in their sexual development towards adulthood, with every developmental stage requiring a different approach. Throughout the book, you will notice that we use the phrase 'age' or 'developmentally appropriate' because children of the same age are often at different developmental levels so age can only ever be a guide.

It is worth emphasizing, at this point, that talking with your children about sexuality will not encourage them to have sex. In fact, research shows that talking about relationships and sexuality with children and young people often results in delayed sexual debut.[1, 2]

In this book, we follow the line of a growing group of experts who promote a positive approach to sexuality education. This means that instead of focusing on preventing problems, risks and unhealthy situations in the sexual and relational life of our children and adolescents, positive sexuality education should place greater emphasis on the more positive aspects. If we reflect, just for a moment, on the messages we, as adults, might have received in sexuality education when we were growing up and on how we generally talk about sexual issues with children and adolescents, the messages are usually negative. We tend to give warnings to children; we tell them *not* to do certain things, we tell them how to avoid sexual harassment and abuse and how to protect themselves against unwanted pregnancies and infections. We forget to tell them that age-appropriate sexual relationships and behaviours are natural, human and an important part of life. We certainly tend to skip the part that says that sexual relationships can be enjoyable because we don't want children and young people to become curious and to start to experiment with these kinds of behaviours. But what kind of messages do we give children if we give them relationships and sexuality education like that? We tell them to be afraid, to be prepared for problems and that sex is risky and dangerous.

We think that this is not an honest message to give to our children. Positive sexuality education aims to change the tone of relationships and sexuality education to become more positive. That is not to say that telling children and adolescents about risks and possible problems is unimportant, but the story should not only be about this. The emphasis of positive relational and sexuality education is on how everyone can and has the right to enjoy their relationships and sexuality in their own way as long as it does not hurt or harm anyone. This book is written with these values in mind. Positive sexuality education is also called empowering sexuality education, and this is the aim of this book; we want to empower children to enjoy their own sexuality in a safe and healthy way.

An important note to repeat here is that positive sexuality is not about promoting sexual behaviour to young children nor is it just about promoting the positive sides of relationships and sexuality. Part of a positive approach is that it should be clear that one way to enjoy relationships and sexuality is knowing how to avoid and prevent risks and problems. A useful analogy is teaching a child how to ride a bike. We tell them how to do it and we encourage them when they do it right. But we also tell them to take care on a busy street, that they cannot cross a dangerous highway and that they have to wear a helmet to prevent them being injured if they fall, and if they'd rather walk or not ride a bike, that's fine too. We don't just tell them they cannot do it because it is fraught with danger!

How should I use this book?

Wherever you are in the world and whatever your role, this book is intended to provide you with evidence-based information about the sexual development of children and how to guide this specific aspect of child development. Although the book is underpinned by research, we have made it practical and easy to use for everyone, regardless of whether you are new to this type of conversation or it is your profession. To get the most out of the book we suggest that you read it in chapter order but if you are more interested in the topic in general we recommend that you focus on Chapter 1, which explores how well you know the child or children that you have in mind when reading this book, Chapter 2, which discusses the challenges and opportunities in adult-child sexuality communication, and Chapter 3, which introduces tips for communicating with children about relationships and sexuality. If you are more interested in getting background information about the social, emotional and sexual development of children, we recommend that you read Chapter 4 and that you go to Chapters 5 to 8 for guidance about how to discuss specific topics at the different ages and developmental stages. If you have concerns about determining what healthy sexual behaviour is and isn't, you will find Chapter 9 particularly useful. In the final chapter, we encourage you to reflect on your learning, and suggest sources for additional support.

We hope that you will enjoy this book, but above all, we hope that you learn that relationships and sexuality education is important and that it can be less difficult and awkward than you might expect – it can even be fun!

Enjoy the book and get in touch with us to share your stories (https://blog.jkp.com).

Chapter 1

Being in Touch with Your Child

Life is busy, with so many competing pressures, that we rarely get the opportunity to reflect on something as simple as the following question: How well do I know my child? But this question is key to establishing the building blocks for relationships and sexuality education. So, read on and, when prompted, answer our questions truthfully and without self-judgement. At times, the focus of this chapter will be on the family and parents, but all of the discussions can be applied to other settings and other adult-child relationships.

A 'warm family climate'

Research suggests that children who grow up in a 'warm family climate'[1] are happier, have greater confidence and experience healthier sexual development than children who do not live in this kind of environment. By healthy sexual development we are referring to children growing up content with their sexuality and sexual feelings and empowered with knowledge to take healthy and responsible decisions concerning their sexuality with respect to others.

But what do the researchers mean by a 'warm family climate'? The term describes an environment in which a child is surrounded by people who are interested in them and who are aware of what is going on with them – if they are happy or sad, worried or scared, depressed or motivated and so on. If a child has adults in their life who show this kind of interest, they are likely to feel safe and comfortable and will be more willing to share their worries, questions and experiences related to relationships and sexuality with the adults around them. In turn, they are more likely to receive support and guidance in this aspect of their development. This may seem obvious but it is worth highlighting since many of us have extremely busy lives with demanding jobs, busy households and parents to take care of, which can make sitting down with a child and listening to their story difficult to achieve.

If you have children of pre-school age or care for or work with this age group, discussions around relationships and sexuality may not seem relevant yet to you. We believe, however, that a child is never too young to receive sexuality education that is relevant for their age or stage of development. The reasons for this will become clearer throughout the book. But showing an interest every day in how children feel, what they've been doing and what they like or dislike is the minimum they need, regardless of age. This doesn't mean that adults need to know every detail of a child's life though. It is up to the child to keep certain things private and it is a child's choice as to how much they want to share with you. But a child who experiences trust, loyalty and, above all, a non-judgemental attitude from a parent, teacher or carer is more willing to share intimate and personal issues and questions.

A quick test

Let's do a quick test to help you see how well you really know the children in your care. Try to answer all the questions that are relevant to the children's stages of development. Keep your notes safe as we'll ask you to repeat the test after completing the book and you'll need to compare your two sets of answers. Throughout the questions, we have referred to the child or children you'll be thinking of as 'they' but you may be thinking about just one child, perhaps your little girl or granddaughter or you may be thinking about a whole class full of children or perhaps a caseload – just personalize the questions to you and your context:

1. Do you know the names of three children they have a good relationship with?

   a. Yes, the names are...

   b. I know just one name, but not any others

   c. No, I don't know any names

2. Do you know when they are unhappy at school or pre-school?

   a. Yes

   b. Sometimes

   c. No

3. Do you talk every day about what happened at school or pre-school?

   a. Yes, every day

   b. Sometimes

   c. No, hardly ever

4. Do you know what they are doing on social media? (If they are too young for social media, just skip this question.)

   a. Yes, exactly

   b. Not everything, but enough

   c. No, that is private for them

5. Do you know what they already know about sexuality?

    a. At least everything I have told them

    b. Not much, they are too young for this

    c. I don't know what they know

6. Do you ever talk with them about relationships and sexuality?

    a. Yes

    b. Never

7. If they have questions about relationships and sexuality issues, do they know where to get answers?

    a. Yes, they come to me

    b. I assume they know

    c. I don't know where they get their information from

8. Do you have any books available for them to learn about relationships and sexuality?

    a. Yes

    b. No

9. If you were to discover they have a problem with sexuality or if they demonstrate problematic sexual behaviour, do you know where to go to for help?

    a. Yes, I know

    b. No, I don't know

10. Do you know their opinions about teenage pregnancy, contraception, sexual diversity and masturbation? (If they are too young for these topics, just skip this question.)

    a. Yes, because we talk about these things

    b. I have no idea what they think about these topics

Your answers

Many of the 'a' answers refer to the various emotional aspects of children's lives. So, the more times you answered 'yes' to 'a', the closer your emotional bond with the child and the closer you are to having what the researchers call a 'warm family climate'. Your answers will have been shaped by your attitudes, values and beliefs. Additionally, they will have been influenced by your parenting or educating style.

Parenting styles or educating styles

For the purposes of this book we have extended the term 'parenting styles' to apply to how parents, carers and professionals interact with children. We therefore use the terms 'parenting styles' and 'educating styles' synonymously in this context.

A lot has been written about parenting or educating styles and which approach is more effective. One of the most influential psychologists to write about different parenting styles and their influence on children's personality development was Diana Baumrind.[2] This American psychologist identified three main parenting styles:

1. *Authoritarian:* the authoritarian parenting style is characterized by high demandingness with low responsiveness.

2. *Permissive:* this parenting style is characterized by low demandingness with high responsiveness.

3. *Authoritative:* this parenting style is characterized by high demandingness with high responsiveness. The authoritative parent is firm but not rigid and willing to make an exception when the situation warrants. The authoritative parent is responsive to the child's needs but not indulgent.

Baumrind makes it clear that she favours the authoritative style and a Dutch study has demonstrated that the authoritative style is most supportive of children and adolescents' healthy sexual development.[3, 4] In this study, it was found that parental support and knowledge about the main aspects of the child's life were the main contributors to healthy sexual development (better use of contraception, better social skills, first sexual intercourse at an older age). Both aspects – support and knowledge – play a role in authoritative parenting.[3, 4]

More recently, psychologist John Gottman[5] identified four parenting styles based on the theory of 'emotional intelligence' put forward by Daniel Goleman.[6] John Gottman promotes the 'emotion coach' style in supporting children to become empathetic people who are aware of their own and others' emotions.

1. *The Dismissing Parent:* In this parenting style, the child's emotions are considered unimportant and are often ignored. When the child shows a negative emotion, such as crying, sadness or anger, the dismissing parent tends to want these emotions to disappear quickly and they may associate

emotional expression as manipulative. Events that trigger emotions in the child are seen as unimportant or ignored, and the child receives no support in addressing the underlying problem.

2. *The Disapproving Parent:* In this style, parents demonstrate similar behaviours to those described above, but they are framed more negatively. The disapproving parent may be critical of the child's emotions, and tends to want the child to conform to certain standards of behaviour and control negative emotions. Emotions are perceived as a sign of weakness, unproductive and a waste of time, and it is believed that children need to be emotionally robust to survive.

3. *The Laissez-Faire or Neglecting Parent:* In contrast to the styles above, this style is accepting of all emotional expression on the part of the child. Little or no guidance is given and no boundaries are set. The belief is that the best way to deal with negative emotions is to let the child release them. This style does not support the child in learning to solve the problem underlying the emotion.

4. *The Emotion Coach Parent:* This style is respectful of the child's emotions. Feelings are not ignored or judged; instead negative emotions are seen as an opportunity to become closer to the child and show empathy and affection. The child's emotions are valued and they will not be told how they should feel by the parent. Instead, the child is helped with labeling the emotion and offered guidance in regulating and expressing strong negative emotions. The child will also be supported in solving the underlying problem.

This last style supports children in learning to trust their feelings, regulate their own emotions and solve problems. Consequently, they are more likely to have high self-esteem, learn well and get along well with others.

Your style

Do you want to know what kind of parenting style you use? John Gottman has developed a questionnaire for parents and caregivers to test their parenting or educating style. You can find this test on his website.*

Being in touch

Have you noticed that very little of the discussion so far has touched on relationships and sexuality? This is because how we communicate about relationships and sexuality is simply a natural extension of how we go about every other aspect of adult-child communication. If children feel supported and safe with you in their everyday lives, they will feel supported and safe in learning about more sensitive issues with you too.

So, a key aspect of relationships and sexuality education is concerned with being in touch with our behaviours as parents, carers and professionals. Another key area is being in touch with the realities of children's lives. Below we have summarized a few facts about children's lives today.

---

* Website: www.johngottman.com. Questionnaire: www.gottman.com/blog/what-style-of-parent-are-you

Things that make children happy

Research commissioned by UNICEF UK,[7] with children aged eight to twelve in the UK, Spain and Sweden, aimed to identify what makes children happy. The families and children in each country told the researchers that spending time with people they loved such as their friends, family and pets, being outdoors and doing fun activities made them happy. The children rarely mentioned their possessions when describing what made them happy and when they were asked to express their preference between having everything they want but little time with their parents and lots of time with their parents but not always having what they want, the vast majority chose more time with their parents.

A further study by UNICEF[8] demonstrated that when international comparisons are made about the wealth of a country and children's well-being, the wealth of a country does not necessarily mean that children are happier. For instance, out of a league table of 29 of the world's richest countries, the US was ranked 26th, Canada 17th and the UK 16th for their children's overall well-being. Factors such as the quality of family relationships appear to play a much greater role in explaining variations in children's perceptions of well-being than materialistic factors.[9]

Romantic love

We know that children, even young children, can experience feelings of romantic love. Our years of experience with parents, teachers and other educators give us enough evidence to know that even children in kindergarten can experience feelings of love or have a crush on another person. In a study in the Netherlands,[10] more than half of the eight- to nine-year-olds who participated said they were in love/had a crush on someone or had been in love or had a crush previously. In another study,[11] almost 80 per cent of the children who participated had experienced feelings of love or attraction for another child by the age of 12. An important point to highlight here is that this does not mean that these children were intending to have sex. Romantic feelings do not have to be directly related to sexual behaviours. This is one of the messages of Dutch sexuality education. Indeed, Dutch children have sex later than their international counterparts.[11]

Pornography

This may seem a strange topic to include in this book given that the children we are referring to are very young. However, we know that young children are, on occasion, exposed to pornography. For example, a research team in the US[12] conducted an online survey with 279 US parents who had a child who had seen pornography when they were less than 12 years old. Sixty-nine per cent reported that as far as they were aware their child's pornography viewing was unintentional, 6 per cent weren't sure and 24 per cent stated that their child had intentionally viewed pornographic material. Similarly, research in the UK[13] with 2284 parents and children demonstrated that 51 per cent of 11–13-year-olds reported that they had seen pornography, with the majority (62%) saying that they had stumbled across it unintentionally. Children described feeling 'grossed out' and 'confused', or reported not understanding what they had seen or being indifferent, particularly those who had seen pornography when they were under the age of ten.

Sexual abuse or harassment

Sadly, sexual abuse of children is common across all cultures and communities. There is a wide variation in the estimates of the number of children who are the victims of sexual abuse. This stems from differences in how abuse is defined, the time periods over which studies are conducted and the fact that many cases of child sexual abuse are never reported. Despite these challenges, it is clear that childhood sexual abuse occurs in every country.

In the US, for example, research estimates that about one in four girls and one in six boys experience some form of child sexual abuse at some point in childhood.[14] It is important to note that more then 90 per cent of child sexual abuse is perpetrated by someone the child knows.[15] Although this makes uncomfortable reading, it is essential that we do not assume that every child's home is a safe space for them. We will return to sexual abuse later in the book.

Reality check

The information that you have just read can be quite shocking. For example, many adults will have no idea that children as young as ten may have already watched porn, but this is a reality for some. It may not be for your child or the children in your care, but it will definitely be for some other children who they may come into contact with or be friends with. Also, if you work with children, you are very likely to have worked with abused children and with children who will face abuse in their future. This is why communication with children, showing an interest in their daily lives and how they are feeling, is absolutely vital.

Summary

We hope that this chapter has got you thinking about your beliefs, attitudes and values concerning children's relationships and sexuality education. We also hope that it has made you think about your behaviours in relation to parenting or educating styles. And finally, we hope that we have tuned you in to the realities of some children's lives.

Throughout this book, we will provide tips to support you in communicating about relationships and sexuality in an age-appropriate way. For many adults, these are the most difficult topics to communicate with children about, and for some, it seems unnecessary to discuss these issues with young children at all. In the next chapters, we will explain why it is important to start communicating about these topics as early as possible and how you can do this.

Chapter 2

Challenges and Opportunities in Discussing Sexuality with Children

When the words *children*, *sexuality* and *education* are included in the same sentence, heated debate often ensues. Common responses are: 'Young children don't need to know about these things', 'Children shouldn't know about such an adult topic' and, sometimes, 'If you tell them, they'll start experimenting'. Do these fears sound familiar to you? In this chapter, we're going to help you debunk the myths and confusion surrounding this important aspect of child development.

Sex or sexuality?

A good place to start in addressing these controversies is to explore the concept of sexuality. Here's an exercise:

Write 'sexuality' in the centre of a piece of paper. What was the first thing that came into your mind when you read that word?

Your first thought may have been love or a behaviour (either negative or positive) like kissing or touching, or perhaps you thought of sexual orientation. All of these responses are right because every person has their own ideas about what sexuality means and there is no single 'right' definition. Now develop your thoughts further by completing the following exercise:

Develop a mind map with the term 'sexuality' in the centre and write down everything that comes to mind when you think of the concept.

Your responses may have been limited or far-reaching, depending on your background and context. To help you expand your thinking further, we have listed the various aspects of sexuality below, drawing from the international literature.

Sexuality encompasses the following aspects:

- Physical: our bodies, how we look and express ourselves, age-related changes to our bodies.

- Emotional: love, attraction, happiness, pleasure, jealousy, disappointment, sadness, nervousness, sexual arousal.

- Relational: bonds between two (or more) people, marriage, friendship.

- Behavioural: kissing, hugging, touching, holding hands, writing messages, sexual intercourse or other sexual behaviours (alone or with others), sexual harassment, abuse.

- Consequences of behaviours: happiness, pregnancy, infection, abortion.

- Gender: gender stereotypes, gender identity, gender fluidity, sexual identity, sexual orientation, LGBTIQ (lesbian, gay, bisexual, transgender/transsexual, intersex and queer/questioning).

- Cultural: ideas about sexuality that vary among different cultures.

- Religious: beliefs about masturbation, abortion, sex before marriage or the purpose of intercourse (e.g. reproduction).

- Legal: age of consent, laws about sexual relationships between adults and children.

- Values: what is right or wrong, appropriate or inappropriate.

Sex education or sexuality education?

As you can see, sexuality is so much more than sexual intercourse, but many adults conflate sexuality with sexual behaviour (or specifically with sexual intercourse). There is, therefore, a common misconception that sexuality education is the same as sex education. But, in the same way that sex is just one aspect of sexuality, sex education is only one aspect of sexuality education.

Comprehensive sexuality education (CSE) focuses on much more than sex.

Comprehensive sexuality education covers a broad range of issues relating to both the physical and biological aspects of sexuality and the emotional and social aspects. It recognizes and accepts all people as sexual beings and is concerned with more than just the prevention of disease or pregnancy. CSE programmes should be adapted to the age and stage of development of the target group.[1]

Adult sexuality versus children's sexuality

There is a big difference between adult sexuality and children's sexuality. For many adults, sexuality is related to sexual feelings, such as sexual arousal and to sexual behaviours. For children, however, sexuality is not related to these things at all. Children are certainly curious about their bodies and they may enjoy the sensation of touching their bodies and their genitals, but they do not relate this feeling to sexual attraction or sexual behaviour. They don't even know that this feeling is sexual, they just consider it exciting, comforting or nice.[2, 3]

The difference between adults' perceptions and understandings of sexuality and those of children is vitally important when we consider sexuality education for young children. For children, learning about sexuality is similar to learning about anything else, since sexuality does not have the same connotations as it does for adults. As one parent said to us: 'For children, learning about reproduction is the same as learning about travelling to the moon – it's just another set of facts, it's not going to make them horny!'

Addressing fears

We hope the above discussions will have addressed two of the major concerns you or other adults around you may have about relationships and sexuality education for children:

- Relationships and sexuality education is *not* about teaching children how to have sexual intercourse.

- Children do *not* associate sexuality with sex in the same way that many adults do.

However, some adults also fear that sexuality education may adversely affect their children in some way. This fear is totally unfounded and, in fact, it is quite the contrary. We now know that sexuality education, even at a very young age, when done properly in an age- and developmentally appropriate way, will lead to more knowledgeable children and adolescents who are better able to protect themselves against unwanted sexual encounters and they will also be better equipped to make well-informed decisions about their own sexual life as they mature.[4] Moreover, when the information is given in a positive way, children and adolescents are better equipped to make positive choices related to their own and others' sexual development, not only knowing what they don't want but, importantly, knowing what they do want.

Values

Values are a very important aspect of sexuality education and it is important that, as a parent, carer or an educator, you are aware of your own values and which ones you wish to convey to the child or children in your care. Here's an exercise that aims to encourage you to take some time to reflect on your own values. The list has come from professionals and parents with whom we have worked over the years. Have a look at the table below and decide which statements you agree or disagree with.

	AGREE	DISAGREE
Sex and love belong together		
Every person has the right to experience sexuality in their own way as long as it is not harmful for others		
Boys and girls are equal		
Boys and girls are different from birth and should be treated differently		
Young girls look better in dresses		
Sexual behaviour with a partner should be delayed until marriage		
Sexual behaviour is something for adults when they love each other very much		
Sexual behaviour is for grown-ups and can happen even when there is no love		
People have different sexual desires and needs		

Everyone has the right to express their sexuality in any way they want as long as it doesn't harm another person		
We should respect another person's boundaries		
We need to be clear as to what our boundaries are		
We should not feel shame for having sexual feelings		
We should not feel embarrassed for not having sexual feelings		
Fathers should be involved in sexuality education for both their sons and daughters		
Sexual diversity is a normal part of sexuality education		
Homosexuality is okay, even for my own child		
Sexuality education is not appropriate for children under 11 years old		
It is better to start to discuss sexuality with children from a young age		
Sexuality education should be taught to girls and to boys separately		

Our personal opinions and our values about relationships and sexuality education can have a significant influence on what we convey to children when discussing relationships and sexuality. Children need clear, factually accurate information. By being aware of our opinions and values related to relationships and sexuality we are better able to distinguish between facts and what we personally believe.

Although we have referred to parents and educators synonymously throughout the book so far, when considering values, the two roles deviate slightly. The educator's role is to help children to understand an issue and to develop their own personal ideas about the topic, whereas parents might also wish to convey their personal or family values to their child. Parents absolutely have the right to do this and it is part of their role. For professional educators, though, our advice would be to focus on factual information as much as possible, to explain that different people will have different values and to encourage children to develop their own values and opinions as much as possible, based on factual information they receive from you.

The impact of our own experiences

Regardless of whether you are a parent or an educator, it is also important to reflect on your personal experiences of relationships and sexuality because these are likely to influence the way you talk to your child. A simple example relates to how you might talk to your child or, if you are a teacher, your class about menstruation. If you are a woman who has struggled with a lifetime of menstrual cramps, you may find that your explanation goes beyond the factual explanation of the non-fertilized egg needing to leave the female body to include reference to pain or discomfort. Likewise, if you are a father or a male teacher, you may find that your observations of how your mother, sister, girlfriend or wife have experienced their periods may become a part of the factual explanation.

Your own sexuality education may also influence your views on sexuality and sexuality education for children. Even if you had no sexuality education at all, even if your parents or teachers never talked about these topics, you will have picked up certain messages, for example: 'These issues are embarrassing', 'Children don't need to know about this', 'Sexuality is dirty' and so on. If this is your experience, you may be motivated to be completely different from your own parents in this regard, but you may find it difficult to broach these subjects with your child. If the latter applies to you, the good news is that by simply being aware of where your reservations come from, you will be better placed to convey more positive messages.

You may also have reservations about having sexuality-related conversations with your child if you have had negative experiences of relationships and sexuality. One of us once received a letter from a mother of a five-year-old girl, asking for advice on how to give sexuality education to her daughter in such a way that she would not become afraid of intimate encounters later in life. The mother had a history of sexual abuse and for her, sexuality had very negative connotations. She wrote: 'I am so afraid that she might have negative experiences like I did. So, the only way I can talk about sex is to tell her not to engage at all with boys and men when she grows up.' Our answer to the mother was as follows:

Dear x,

It is completely understandable that your own experiences with men and with sex have made you fearful for your daughter's sexual life in the future. Of course you want to protect her. Being aware that your views on sexuality and sexuality education are influenced by your own experiences and values is the first step to becoming a good sexuality educator. The next step is to reflect on these thoughts and to formulate for yourself what important values and messages you want to give your daughter. We know from research that children who grow up in a safe environment and are able to express their emotions to their parents or trusted adults are better protected against sexual abuse than children who do not feel safe and who never learn how to share their worries with someone they trust. If you can provide this kind of environment for your daughter, you will already be doing a good job as a parent. If you can give your daughter the self-confidence to trust her own instincts when dealing with uncertain or threatening situations, you will have done a truly excellent job as a parent. To teach her self-confidence is much better than giving her warnings about risky situations she might experience, since warning messages make children afraid and anxious…

The point here is that we should try to not let our personal histories have a negative impact on our children's development.

If there's a void a child will fill it

Children can be smart and intuitive. If they learn that adults do not want to talk about sexuality-related topics with them, they will quickly stop asking questions and they will go elsewhere for their information – perhaps to their friends or the internet, or they might just create their own answers. This is probably not what you want.

Most young children can access the internet and they can readily find answers to their questions, but it is unlikely that these will be suitable, age- and developmentally appropriate answers. Sexuality is everywhere today, in all kinds of media. As we established in Chapter 1, some primary school children will have already watched pornography and we also know that increasing numbers of primary school children are accessing social media; for example, research in the UK estimated that 59 per cent of children had started using social media before the age of 10.[5]

If we do not communicate about relationships and sexuality with our children from an early stage and leave them to find out in their own way, we make them vulnerable. While these conversations are not always easy, it is our duty as adults to support children in this aspect of their development.

'But my child never asks'

This is a common quote from parents that we meet. Even if children do not ask questions about sexuality, it does not necessarily mean that they are not curious. Sometimes they simply do not know how to express their feelings or they do not yet have the right words. As we have already outlined, children who know that the adults in their lives are willing to answer their questions about sexuality will feel safer to ask such questions. However, you may well be an extremely approachable adult but a child may still rarely ask questions about sexuality. If this is the case, continue to create a supportive environment by giving caring attention, listening to what they have to say, asking them questions about how they feel and about their activities, by reading together, looking at pictures in books together and by cuddling when they want a cuddle. In doing this, you will create the warm atmosphere we discussed in Chapter 1, in which you can start to discuss topics related to sexuality. In the next chapters, we will discuss how to do this, but the point to make here is that children who never ask questions do still have questions.

It is your task as an educator to help children in your care to find words for what they feel, and it is your task as a sexuality educating parent to closely monitor your child to see if they are ready to listen to what you have to tell them about sexuality.

Remember to keep in mind this important rule: always answer every question that a child asks about sexuality, even if the question is difficult or embarrassing. It's perfectly okay to tell a child that you find their questions difficult; children have no problem with that. But try to formulate an answer, even if it is very simple. And if you don't know the answer straightaway, tell them that you will find out the answer and come back to them with it, but make sure that you do!

Children's rights

A brief word about children's rights. In 1989, world leaders made a historic commitment to the world's children by adopting the United Nations Convention on the Rights of the Child – an international agreement on childhood. It has become the most widely ratified human rights treaty in history and has helped transform children's lives around the world. These rights for children were developed to ensure their personal, physical, emotional and mental development and to protect them from harm.

One of these rights is the 'right to education'. If we define education as meaningful, age-appropriate information to guide a child's development, information about relationships and sexuality is highly relevant to fulfilling this right. Another important child's right is the 'right to be protected'. Children should be protected against any physical and mental harm, including sexual harm. Sexual abuse and sexual harassment have an enormous impact on the development of a child and often continue to have adverse effects through to adulthood. We know that comprehensive sexuality education has a protective effect on a child's development in relation to the prevention of sexual abuse and harassment.[4] Good sexuality education gives children the words to express when they feel uncomfortable in a specific sexual situation. It also gives children information about what can be considered healthy or harmful for a child in the context of sexual situations. It can also make children feel empowered and it gives them confidence about their body and their right to refuse or to say 'no' when feeling threatened or uncomfortable. Children also learn where to go for help and support. In other words, sexuality education, when given in a group or individually, fulfils several important universal human rights, even when children are very young.

We want to make it clear, however, that a child is never guilty, not even partially, if they have been sexually abused, whether they have received comprehensive sexuality education or not. They should not be blamed for not telling anybody about the abuse and they should not be made to feel in any way responsible. It must be acknowledged that the risk of sexual abuse remains even when parents, carers and teachers provide children with the best possible sexuality education.

Finally, in keeping with positive relationships and sexuality education, we believe that it is a child's right to learn that sexuality is a natural part of human life and that everyone, regardless of their age, is entitled to enjoy their sexuality in a developmentally appropriate way, as long as it does not harm others. By conveying the positive aspects of relationships and sexuality, alongside the negative sides and possible dangers that a child can encounter, children and adolescents can be empowered to minimize risks in order to enjoy their sexuality in a safe way.

Summary

As we said at the beginning of this chapter, children's relationships and sexuality education can be fraught with controversies. By addressing the key challenges – for example confusion about the meaning of sexuality and sexuality education as opposed to sex and sex education, misunderstandings about adult sexuality versus children's sexuality and common fears – we hope that you are beginning to see that this aspect of child development perhaps isn't so different to other aspects. In the next chapter, we expand on some of these points and discuss how to communicate with children about sexuality-related issues.

Chapter 3

Communicating with Children about Sexuality

When we share our mantra 'start sexuality education with children as young as possible', a very common response from parents, carers and educators of pre-school and primary school children is hesitation and confusion. Common questions include: 'I want to wait until they are a bit older before I talk to them properly. Is that wrong?' and 'What can I tell a little baby? She can't understand what I am saying yet.' These questions are absolutely valid and, in this chapter, we will answer these questions and others to help address both the 'whys' and the 'hows' that our mantra provokes.

Communicating or talking?

Communicating and talking are subtly different. Communication involves both verbal (i.e. talking) and non-verbal communication. When you communicate with children, you might use words, but you will also communicate in non-verbal ways. For example, a teacher may use a certain facial expression when they see a child touching their own genitals, or parents might laugh when two adults kiss on TV or they may imitate their homosexual neighbour in front of their child. In all of these examples, no words will have been spoken, but a message will have been conveyed, such as shock, embarrassment or disapproval. In turn, the child is likely to have made their own interpretations, such as: 'I am doing something wrong when I touch my genitals', 'Adults are stupid when they kiss each other' or 'Mummy doesn't like the neighbour; she is making fun of him.'

Children learn from communication; they learn from all the messages they receive, even when they are very young. Babies learn from their parents' and carers' facial expressions and tone of voice; they do not understand words yet, but they can perceive safety and warmth. They recognize their parents' voices and feel safe and happy when these voices are loving and caring. We know, too, that when a parent is upset, babies also perceive this from the change in voice alone and this may make them unhappy.[1] So, parents and carers share messages about relationships and sexuality from the day a child is born and as the young child's life expands to include kindergarten staff, teachers, other children and other adults they continue to pick up on and assimilate all kinds of messages, including ones about relationships and sexuality. In other words, relationships and sexuality education begins right from birth, even if you have not directly spoken about it! So, the answer to: 'Why should we start sexuality education as young as possible?' is quite simply: 'It is happening already!'

The benefits of starting young

It might be helpful to highlight the benefits of starting sexuality education from a young age, for both children and their parents and carers. Children will:

- learn from a young age that it is acceptable and normal to communicate about sexuality-related topics

- understand that relationships and sexuality are relevant to every age group and every human being

- understand that communicating about these topics doesn't have to lead to guilt, embarrassment or fear

- learn that communicating, especially with words, is important in all relationships.

Parents and carers can:

- convey the values that they think are important for their child to learn

- show their children that communicating about these topics can lead to helpful answers and solutions

- experience a deeper bond with their children as a result of these exchanges

- emphasize the positive aspects of sexuality rather than only giving warnings and fear-based messages

- find it easier to communicate about other aspects of growing up

- discover that communicating about these topics doesn't have to be difficult or embarrassing – it can be very special and even fun!

What happens when a child has no relationships and sexuality education at all?

This is a very important, challenging question. It would be impossible to conduct research to answer this question because it would be ethically unacceptable to deprive children of sexuality education right up to adulthood. So, we cannot give an answer based on research data, but as experts we know that if parents and other significant adults in a child's life do not talk about relationships and sexuality with them, children will pick up on hidden messages and conclude:

'They don't want to talk about this stuff with me.'

'I should look for answers myself.'

'It's abnormal to want to know about these things at my age.'

'It's rude to talk about these things.'

In addition to a lack of spoken communication, the non-verbal messages adults convey may be equally powerful in communicating negative messages. Or they may be conflicting and confusing for children if an adult's behaviours are sexualized but verbal communication about relationships and sexuality is not on offer. For example, children may hear mummy and daddy having sex, or observe flirtatious and sexualized behaviours by one or both parents but if verbal communication about sexuality is prohibited this can cause significant confusion.

For parents and carers, all of these interpretations have the potential to create a barrier between you and your child. In addition, you will be depriving your child of the protective impact that open parent-child sexuality communication can have for children (see previous chapters). So, we suggest that it would be preferable to proactively communicate with your child about relationships and sexuality, rather than leaving their education to chance. As we highlighted earlier, this will not only be beneficial for your child but it will also benefit you! And for teachers, if you can encourage an open dialogue about relationships and sexuality in the classroom, you will be giving the children in your care a tremendous gift that they will carry with them throughout their lives.

Which parent?

Returning to parents and carers for a moment, in families with more than one parent or carer, there is often debate as to which parent should take on the role of sexuality educator. Our opinion is that whatever kind of family a child grows up in, whether there is one, two or more parents, it's best if all parents or carers are involved in their own way in sexuality education, whatever the gender of the parent. However, we know from research[2] that in western countries females are more likely to be responsible for the general education of their child or children. From Dutch studies,[3] we know that with respect to sexuality education, most children turn to their mothers to ask questions and that, in most families, the mother is the one who provides information about sexuality and relationships. That doesn't mean that the other parent has no part in this kind of education though. What we see, at least in the Netherlands and other western countries, is that mothers are more active in verbal sexuality education and fathers in non-verbal relationships and sexuality education.[4] It doesn't matter who tells the child the verbal story of relationships and sexuality, as both parents contribute in their own way.

But what about children who live in a one-parent family or with two parents of the same sex, or maybe with three or four parents? With regards to the child's relationships and sexuality education, it doesn't matter where a child grows up, as long as their carer(s) creates a warm, open, non-judgemental atmosphere in which the child can feel loved, wanted and important.[5] If children know that they are allowed to ask questions about sexuality and as long as they feel that regardless of what they ask or do in relation to sexuality their carers will always accept them as their child, the composition of the child's family does not matter.

Okay, but how?

For very specific tips on how to explain certain topics to children at different ages, have a look at Chapters 5–8. There, we elaborate on specific words and expressions suitable for different age groups and we provide several examples of conversations. However, the following general tips will make communication about relationships and sexuality easier and more comfortable for both you as a parent, carer or educator and the children in your care, regardless of their age.

Top tips

Always answer every question

By asking a question, children are showing you that they are interested in a particular topic. Regardless of what has prompted the question and whether you are shocked by it or consider it inappropriate or too mature for their age, it is still important to answer the question. Avoid dodging the question with counter questions like, 'Why do you want to know?' and don't 'forget' to give a reply if you promise to discuss the issue later or if you need to look the answer up.

Keep it short and simple

If a child under five years of age wants to know how a baby is made, don't bother giving a Wikipedia-length answer. They just need a simple, short response. For the child, this question won't be a big deal, although it may be for you! In Chapters 5–8 we give some examples of short, simple answers for these kinds of questions.

Find the right moment ('talkable' moments)

If a child doesn't seem interested in any of the topics that sexuality encompasses, but you think it's time to start giving them some information, seek out some 'talkable' moments. For example, you could use a scene from a TV series, an advertisement, something in the news or you could make reference to someone you both know. Examples for families might be: 'Did you hear that Auntie Jane is pregnant? What do you think will happen in her tummy?' Or perhaps, if you watch a sanitary towel or tampon advert together on the TV, you might ask: 'Do you know why women have to use sanitary towels and tampons?' A useful tip for having these types of conversations is to avoid sitting opposite the child, so you have to face each other. If a child is embarrassed by the topic, they will feel even more embarrassed if they have to face you and make eye contact with you. It's better to sit next to each other and better still if you can be engaged in some other neutral activity while you talk such as driving, sitting and watching TV or cooking together.

Use simple language

Children who ask a question need an answer they can understand. If the question is about sexuality, particularly reproduction, adults tend to answer in medical terms, using words like uterus, scrotum, ejaculation, coitus. But, younger children, especially those under ten, do not understand these words and will become bored and disinterested in what you are saying. Instead, just use words that children understand. Sometimes a medical word may be necessary, but make sure you check that they understand and, if not, just explain in simple language.

Be approachable rather than judgemental

Reacting in a judgemental way, by saying things like: 'Who taught you words like that?' or 'Don't ask me stuff like that!' may make a child feel that their questions or behaviours are naughty or wrong. Consequently, they may decide to stop asking you questions. Although it's not easy to hide your feelings when you are shocked, it's very important that you pause and compose yourself before responding and if you just can't find the right words, you can get back to the child at another time.

Be curious

Be curious about what children are doing and feeling. This can be just in general, for example parents might ask: 'How was your day?', 'What song are you singing?' or 'Who's that new friend?' If your child is playing games on their mobile phone, you could ask them to teach you the game so that you can play it too. If they want to watch a movie with their classmate, ask them afterwards what part they enjoyed most and why. You can show this same kind of curiosity when young children are discovering their own bodies and emotions, for example you might ask: 'What do you like most about your friendship with…?' or 'How do you feel when you say you want to marry George?' or 'Do you like it when Sara holds your hand?' Parents who display this kind of interest in their children show them that they take their emotional world seriously. By achieving this, you will be showing your children that they can trust you, and, in turn, because they trust you they will be more willing to open up when either of you wants to talk about sexuality.

Ensure your values align with your behaviour

If adults emphasize gender equality to children, but, at the same time, disapprove of boys wanting to grow their hair long or playing with a doll's house, they are conveying inconsistent messages. The same applies when adults tell children that 'gay people are okay', but they also ridicule gay people. Consistency between words and behaviour is extremely difficult and almost everyone has fallen into this inconsistency trap at least once in their life. Opinions and principles are much easier to talk about than enact. Ensuring that our words and actions are consistent takes time and self-reflection. In the next chapters, we will return to this theme in more detail when we discuss stage-specific messages related to sexual development.

Be prepared for tricky questions (and don't be afraid of them)

Children, especially under-fives, are very curious and have many questions about the world around them. Their social skills are not yet fully developed, which means they have no filter as to which topics are sensitive or taboo. What we perceive to be acceptable and not acceptable to discuss in public is influenced by our culture and context. For some people, it is absolutely fine to ask questions about sex and sexuality, money, politics, personal/family issues and so on, whereas for others it isn't. Children have to learn these social rules, and this type of social learning isn't fully developed until around four or five years of age. Young children will, therefore, ask others about everything without embarrassment. As we have already said, it is important that you answer these questions, but it is also perfectly acceptable for you to explain that there is a time and a place for these types of conversations.

Use books as a starting point

If you're not sure where to start, age-appropriate books about relationships and sexuality can make it easier for you. Reading together is a great way to bond, even when the topic is sensitive and difficult. You might want to choose story books that convey a theme or more factual books, or perhaps funny books. Using books means that you don't have to look for the words yourself as the words are in the book and if these words are embarrassing, you can just blame the author! As an example, we recommend any of the books by Cory Silverberg or Todd Parr.

Explain to girls what happens to boys, and vice versa

When boys understand about girls' development, they have greater empathy for girls and the same applies when girls understand how boys develop and mature. These understandings can also underpin future relationships in adulthood as understanding each other's sexual and reproductive development can help build empathy and a willingness to care for each other.

Try to avoid too much emphasis on binary gender

Some children, young people and adults do not consider themselves as a boy/man or a girl/woman. Try to avoid using terms like he/she or him/her and use, if possible, more neutral terms like 'they' and 'them'. When a child wonders if someone is a boy or girl or man or woman, it is better to avoid assuming you know, but explain that you cannot always read someone's gender from the way they look or dress and instead it is better to depend more on how people identify themselves.

Take children seriously

Being dismissive of children's romantic feelings is hurtful and humiliating for them and it tells them that you do not take them seriously. Kindergarten children who say they are in love and want to marry each other really feel this. They want to express their special feelings and at that age they have no other words than 'I want to marry him.' Acknowledging these feelings and showing understanding is the best an adult can do. Of course, it's fine to tell them that they will have to wait several years before they are allowed to marry but let them know that you are happy for them to have these feelings.

Count to ten

'We've played mummy and daddy together and now we want to make a baby. How can we do that?', 'Can I watch you and daddy making love together?' or 'Can I kiss you like adults kiss?' All of these questions are possible and common but they can be quite a shock! Try not to react immediately, count to ten, take a deep breath and say: 'Well…I can tell you how babies are made, but only adults do that. Children can't make babies. Instead, you can pretend. You can put a doll under your top to pretend you're pregnant. Is that okay for you? Let me know if you want to know more about how adults make a baby. Okay?' Most children under six won't be interested in wanting to know any more once they know how they can pretend. For the other questions, you just need to calmly say: 'No, you can't. Making love is for adults and it is private.' If you want to say more and the child wants to hear more, you can explain in simple words how a baby is made (see Chapters 5 and 6).

Practise!

Having these conversations can be awkward for everyone but the more you do it, the more natural it will feel. Try to have simple conversations initially about friendships, boundaries and bodies, starting when children are around three years old or just before. The conversations just need to be short and simple. In Chapters 5–8, we will guide you in several of these conversations and give you some examples that you can use in your own way.

Be self-aware

We don't expect you to suddenly become super confident and comfortable with educating children about relationships and sexuality. You are a product of your own education and history. If you feel very reluctant, listen to your own concerns. If you think, *I definitely can't do this*, just try small steps initially until you feel more confident. As a parent, if you do this while your child is still young, you will feel more at ease by the time your child reaches adolescence. If you wait for the first conversation until adolescence though, it is likely that your reluctance and your child's will probably be too great to overcome.

Stay positive and show your love

This one is for parents and carers but teachers can take something from this too. Have confidence in your ability to become a great parent! Great parents are not born, they are made and learn through experience. Show your love abundantly and in many ways, both in your words and behaviour. This is much more important than your ability to have a good conversation about sexuality!

Summary

What have we covered in this chapter? We have emphasized that communication consists of both verbal and non-verbal communication and we have outlined how children learn about relationships and sexuality from a very young age, even before they are able to understand our words. We have discussed the advantages of communicating with children about relationships and sexuality from an early age and we have briefly touched on some of the risks associated with avoiding such conversations. We have provided some general tips for dealing with awkward questions and prompting these kinds of conversations and we have also discussed parental roles. In the next chapter, we will focus more specifically on children's social and sexual development since an understanding of this underpins age-appropriate communication about relationships and sexuality.

Chapter 4

Social and Sexual Development in Children

As soon as a baby is born, they are a social human being and develop through interaction with their environment. Have you noticed how quickly babies learn how to get attention and approval from their parents or carers? After around six weeks, when most babies start to smile, which is usually just an involuntary movement of the facial muscles, they soon discover that their caregivers will respond positively and lovingly to their smile and will often smile back. They learn that smiling is an important way to connect with others and get positive attention and approval. This learning process is all based on interaction; the child learns from the reactions of others. This is the foundation for their learning about relationships. When children are young, relationships will be concerned with friendships and social contacts but as they mature towards adulthood, relationships may also be intimate or romantic. In this chapter, we will draw on the relevant childhood development theories to discuss how children develop their social skills.

Child development theories

There are many child development theories but, for the purpose of this book, we have limited our focus to the three that we consider to be most relevant for understanding children's development of their social relationships and later intimate relationships: John Bowlby's attachment theory, Erik Erikson's theory on the development of trust in a child and Albert Bandura's four principles of social learning in children. All of these theories are concerned with children's social learning and they are important in helping us understand how children learn to build relationships.

Bowlby's attachment theory

John Bowlby's attachment theory explains that through their interaction with their primary caregiver in the first 18 months of life, babies learn how to attach and relate to others. If the parent or carer provides the baby with enough loving care and fulfils their needs, the baby will build trust and security. They will learn that there is at least one person they can trust and depend on. These children grow up with secure attachment to people they love and in adulthood they have a greater chance of developing secure relationships.

Alternatively, an insecure attachment style can develop when the parent or carer doesn't meet the needs of the child, through neglect, abuse or extreme inconsistency, and where comfort and warmth are unpredictably replaced by rejection.

During childhood, children use their original attachment

patterns when interacting with peers or building relationships with others during their primary school years. Most children are securely attached but some might also show some signs of insecure attachments. On a positive note, signs of insecure attachment can be changed or managed to develop a secure attachment pattern through children's interactions with other caring adults.

Erikson's theory on the development of trust

Erik Erikson's theory on the development of trust in a child outlines stages in which a child develops socially. In each stage, the child learns about social relationships and how they can manage them successfully and satisfactorily. For the purposes of this book, we will focus on the first four stages.

The first stage, which occurs between birth and 18 months, is characterized by building trust with the parent or carer. If the parent or carer is able to give attention and comfort in a satisfactory way, trust in others can be built, which is an important foundation for pleasurable intimate relationships in adolescence and adulthood. In the second stage, between 18 months and three years of age, the child learns to develop autonomy and a sense of personal physical control. Parents and carers who give children the opportunity to experiment with their physical skills and independence stimulate this development of autonomy. The third stage, from three to five years, is characterized by the child learning to take the initiative, through activities like stacking blocks, discovering the outside world or interacting with peers. If these initiatives are rewarded by success, for example the other child agrees to play or the creation of a tall tower, the child will develop a sense of self-control and empowerment over their own skills. The fourth stage, from around six to twelve years, focuses on developing competence. Children at this stage will be learning to read and write, to do sums and to do things on their own. Teachers play an important role in the child's life as they teach the child specific skills. It is at this stage that the child's peer group will become more important and a major contributor to the child's self-esteem. The child now feels the need to win approval by demonstrating specific competencies that are valued by society, and begins to develop a sense of pride in their accomplishments.

Bandura's four principles of social learning

Albert Bandura's four principles of social learning assert that children learn their social skills from: attention, retention, reproduction and motivation. If children see and observe that a specific social behaviour has positive consequences, they are more likely to imitate this behaviour and to expect the same positive result. For instance, if children grow up in a family where emotions are expressed violently, they learn that this is a successful way of getting what you want and might replicate this behaviour in school with their peers, and later in adult relationships.

Prior to around six years of age, children mainly observe, copy and internalize the behaviours of their primary and most important caregivers. But after this age, other caregivers, such as teachers, become role models. Peers and the media become increasingly important in shaping children's social beliefs and behaviour as the years progress.

The realities

As we have established, research consistently demonstrates

how important it is for a child to grow up in a positive, loving, caring and stimulating environment, where a secure attachment is ensured and they have inspiring role models to learn from. However, no parent, carer or teacher can be all of these things, all of the time! We all have our own personal histories and insecurities and we can all be too stressed, hungry or tired to be perfect all of the time. As parents, we know this and we also know that it's okay!

We also know that for many children around the world, the ideal environment described above bears little, if any, resemblance to their experience of childhood. Does this mean that they inevitably face a miserable future full of drugs, violence and other derailments? No, definitely not! Although an early start with physical and/or mental distress gives children an increased risk of developing mental health problems later in life, there are numerous interventions that can prevent or even reverse the damage, even when these interventions don't take place until adulthood. In the back of this book, we have listed websites where you can find out more about child abuse.

Relational and emotional development

The process of learning about relationships is a lengthy one for young children. As we discussed in the introduction to this chapter, babies learn what impact their behaviour has on others from their parents' and other carers' reactions to them. But it is not until a child reaches three to four years of age that they are able to develop real relationships with others. Up to around the age of three, relationships are built on basic principles like trust, kindness and, when related to peers, availability, kindness, smell, attractiveness, voice, clothes and toys.

Until they are approximately three years old, children aren't able to understand what other children feel or think and they are not yet able to meet the needs of another child. Their choices in relation to other children are based only on their own needs. For example, if a two-and-a-half-year-old child is friends with another child, they will think that the other child has the same emotions and thoughts that they have, which makes it difficult for them to understand why the other child might suddenly want their toy or suddenly start to cry when they feel perfectly happy.

Between two and three years of age, Theory of Mind starts to develop very gradually, which means that a child becomes increasingly able to see the perspective of another person. The development of Theory of Mind coincides with the development of a child's identity and concept of self (understanding that they are unique from others). Before a child has developed Theory of Mind, they can play with other children, but it would be more accurate to call it playing *next* to other children. By approximately four years of age, most children will have developed some level of Theory of Mind and will be able to see and understand the perspective of others, and at this stage they will be able to play *with* others. Now they know that their friends might have different emotions from theirs and they understand that when another child starts to cry, that child feels unhappy and needs help.

A child's ability to put themselves in the shoes of another person is extremely important for the development of compassionate empathy and emotional intelligence. As children grow older, they further develop their Theory of Mind. This happens through interaction with others. Parents and carers can do a lot to promote the development of Theory of Mind by using words that refer to thinking and feelings[1, 2] in conversations, for example: 'Did you see Grandma smiling when you gave her that birthday present? She must have felt really happy.' Or by asking children questions such as: 'How do you think your friend would feel if you screamed at her?' or 'How do think your brother feels when you praise him?' By putting feelings into words you can deepen a child's understanding of their own thoughts and feelings and you can demonstrate how others may have different thoughts and feelings from their own. You can also teach them how our behaviours are based on what we think and feel.[3]

However, we must acknowledge here that some children, particularly those with an autism spectrum disorder, can have difficulties with the development of their Theory of Mind. Some can learn to see others' perspectives, but a number will always find it difficult to do this.

Emotional intelligence

An important goal of sexuality education is to educate children in such a way that they are able to form healthy and happy, intimate, romantic and sexual relationships as they progress towards adulthood. Happy and healthy relationships are built on several principles, all related to emotional intelligence. The development of emotional intelligence begins early in life at a very young age. It is concerned with understanding and responding appropriately to our own emotions and the emotions of others.[4]

Children develop emotional intelligence through their interactions with others; initially with their primary caregivers and later with peers and role models. This is why the skill of building friendships and having a good friend is so important for young children. Through friendships, children learn a lot about themselves and others, for example through interacting and dealing with strong emotions such as jealousy or rejection. These are all basic skills that underpin healthy, intimate relationships as a child matures and approaches adulthood. For example, these skills support adolescents in how to say 'yes' and 'no' in their first adolescent relationships. Emotionally intelligent children are also better protected against sexual abuse since they more readily recognize when they feel uneasy about a situation and have greater confidence to get away.[5]

It is, therefore, very important that we talk about emotions with children from a young age. To do this, you could start with the four basic emotions: happy, afraid, angry and sad. Talk to your toddler about how they feel right now, whether they feel happy, afraid, angry or sad, how this feeling makes them feel inside (e.g. does it make them feel relaxed, breathe fast or feel hot?) and you could ask them what emotion they think you are feeling – happy, afraid, angry or sad? As the child grows older, you could gradually move to more complex emotions, like jealousy, excitement, pride, love, loneliness, guilt and confusion.

It can also be helpful to read books with children about emotions and to label their emotions with them as they occur and discuss how the emotion feels. In this way, children learn that feelings have different names and, with time, they will be able to express them with words. This process can be hugely beneficial for children developmentally, since people who are able to share their emotions as adults have better and more stable relationships (in the office, in friendships and in intimate relationships) than people who have difficulty expressing and sharing their feelings.[5]

Empathy

Empathy is the ability to imagine the emotions of another person, almost to the point of feeling the emotions yourself. Empathy plays a crucial role in the social and emotional development of children and in becoming emotionally intelligent. People who are empathic and have emotional intelligence are better able to develop happy and fulfilling intimate relationships later in life.

Daniel Goleman[4] describes three stages in the development of empathy:

1. *Cognitive empathy:* the child is able to understand that someone else may have a different emotion from them and is able to see things from the other person's perspective. This usually starts to develop at around three years of age.

2. *Emotional empathy:* the child is now not only able to understand that someone can have different emotions to them but can also imagine how these emotions feel.

3. *Compassionate empathy:* the child is now able to understand and feel the emotion of another and is immediately willing to help or do something when the emotion is a negative one.

Compassionate empathy is fully developed empathy and it is very useful for children to have developed this by the stage they are starting to develop friendships and deeper relationships. It is also helpful in enabling children to feel comfortable in social situations, like the first day in a new school or when a child moves to another neighbourhood and wants to find new friends. According to Daniel Goleman, children (and adults) who have developed this last stage of empathy can become good team players and good leaders. In this final stage of empathy development, children also know how to manage their own emotions. However, to develop compassionate empathy, a child first needs to develop cognitive and emotional empathy.

Gender identity

The word 'sex' can sometimes be used to refer to the biological differences between males and females, such as the genitalia and genetic differences. 'Gender' is more fluid, but refers to the roles, behaviours, activities, attributes and opportunities that any society considers appropriate for different groups of people. In relation to the nature-nurture discussion, it is now believed that babies are born with a blueprint or predisposition to certain genetically based personality characteristics, but if and how these will be developed in their life depends heavily on the environment in which they grow up. In other words, nurture can impact on nature, particularly with regards to gender identity and expression.

Babies and toddlers learn a great deal about gender simply through how their parents and carers approach them. Take for instance the following example of how we implement an experiment based on the work of Sandra and John Condry:[6]

We let the audience listen to the sound of a baby boy, called David, crying. He cries loudly and intensely. After listening to the cry, we ask the audience to write down what they think baby David is feeling. They write down things like 'very upset' and 'angry'. We write all the feelings and emotions down on a whiteboard and ask participants to choose one overall emotion. They usually agree on 'angry'. 'Okay, great', we say, 'let's listen to another baby cry now and let's try to agree again on one emotion you will hear. This time you will hear a baby girl, Dana. Listen to her cry.' After hearing Dana's crying, they all write down the emotions they hear, such as helplessness and loneliness and they usually come to the agreement that the overall emotion is 'sadness'. As you may have guessed, the cry is identical, the only thing that has changed is the gender label.

In Sandra and John Condry's original experiment they showed pictures of a baby boy (David) and a baby girl (Dana) to parents and asked them to write down the main emotion they saw in the pictures of the babies' faces. The parents saw different emotions depending on the sex of the baby. And, of course, the pictures were of the same baby!

Gender manipulation is shaped by parents and caregivers, who are usually not aware of what they are doing. Parents are better at distinguishing the facial expressions of girls than boys[7] and they talk more to their daughters and use more emotional words than they do with their sons.[8] Parents react faster to a crying daughter and take more time to console her than their sons, and daughters are touched more than sons.[9] Parents also tend to focus on the physical appearance of their daughters and pay more attention to the achievements of their sons.[10] These experiments, and others, demonstrate that adults have different ideas regarding what boys and girls feel and what they want to express or should express. Such beliefs significantly shape children's perceptions of themselves and their expectations of their gender role.

Lawrence Kohlberg's[11] theory of gender development

outlines several stages of children's gender development, with the first stage beginning between two and three years of age, when children are able to label themselves as boys or girls and are able to label others as well. This labelling process is initially based on external, culturally defined physical characteristics such as hair length, lipstick or beards. In addition to these external signs, young children also learn that there is a better characteristic by which to distinguish men and women: their genitals. This discovery is related to the discovery of their own genitals at around the same age and the discovery that others might or might not have the same genitals. Indeed, several years ago one of us went to a colleague's home, wearing trousers, very short hair, earrings and lipstick. A little boy, aged three, opened the door, studied the visitor from top to bottom with a look of confusion and asked: 'Can I see your penis?'

Between three and four years of age, children become curious to see others' genitals and they have many questions: 'Do adult men grow a second penis?', 'Do girls grow a penis when they become women?', 'Why do boys have a penis and girls don't?' and so on. Some become very curious to see other children's and their parents' naked bodies and once a child knows, from the people around them, that they are called a boy or a girl, they start looking around for examples of how they are expected to act and behave. The three-year-old boy imitates his father or big brother's behaviour and clothes, acting in a stereotypical way to be acknowledged by others as a real boy. The same applies to three-year-old girls, with them looking to their mother or older sister to see how they should look and act.

During the first stage of gender identity development, children can still be flexible in their ideas about gender. They know they are called a boy or a girl, but they may fluctuate between their biological sex and another sex for periods of time. For example, it is very common for boys to decide to be the princess and for girls to choose to be the prince while playing. Gender flexibility continues in the second stage of gender development (three to six years old) when most children experience greater gender stability, realizing that they will be a boy or girl forever, but they still think that gender can change during situations such as play. At around six years, many children enter the stage of gender constancy, where they believe that gender will never change in any situation and we see this reflected in children's play, where they stop wanting to play different gender roles. However, we don't know how far this gender constancy is generated by societies which prescribe binary gender or expect everyone to fit into one of two genders, but we do know that some children feel uncomfortable with the biological features they are given at birth. They may feel that their body and identity are out of sync. Biological sex is not the same as gender, and gender is not limited to only two options – gender can be considered as fluid. A person who does not identify as the gender assigned to them by birth is described as transgender. Some people don't identify as male or female but feel, instead, a mix of both genders or neither gender. These people may call themselves 'non-binary', any other label or nothing at all. Gender fluid, agender and genderqueer are all terms that fit under the non-binary category, but each person's experience is unique, so it's best not to apply labels without the permission of the specific person.

In young children, these kinds of feelings may strengthen as they grow up or change. Children's beliefs and behaviours regarding gender will depend on what the environment expects and promotes. If parents and caregivers allow children to experiment and discover different kinds of games, toys and behaviours, they learn that deviating from gendered norms is acceptable. They may also find that this can be fun and pleasurable and, perhaps, more in line with their deepest desires and preferences. Giving children the opportunity and encouragement to explore fully what their individual preferences are, without any judgement, allows them to develop their own talents instead of teaching them to adjust to gendered norms, which can be limiting and counterproductive.

Knowing how to support a transgender or non-binary child in a binary society can be a challenge for some. Knowing more about the diverse spectrum of gender can help parents and educators to adjust their behaviours and language in such a way that all children, regardless of their identity, can feel comfortable.[†]

---

†   We refer here to the wonderful website: www.kidsguidetogender.com (with lots of resources).

Sexual development

Research shows specific age-related behaviours in the development of sexuality in children from western countries. As we have previously stated, we prioritize developmental stage over age as children of the same age can vary so significantly developmentally. The existing research data is age-focused (as well as western-focused) so we have had to use this for reference; however, please do remember that age is only a guide when considering children's development. Below is a short overview of the stages from birth to eleven years, along with the specific behaviours we see at each stage. These behaviours will be explained in more detail in the next four chapters.

Birth to three years: enjoying

- At around six months, some babies experience their first sexual sensation by touching their genitals. This first experience is positive for every child and stays positive as long as the environment does not openly disapprove. Babies and toddlers will not associate these feelings with 'adult sex'.

Four to six years: discovering

- Children learn that everyone has genitals and they become curious to see (and sometimes touch) others' genitals and bodies. It gives them exciting sexual feelings. Children do not associate these feelings with 'adult sex'.

- They discover that they can use language to ask questions related to sexuality and that sometimes adults can become quite upset by these questions.

Seven to nine years: interacting

- By now, they have learned some of the social rules related to sexuality. This means that they will be careful in exposing or touching their genitals in public.

- In their play with others, they sometimes experience very special feelings for someone of another or same sex and this feeling will change their interaction with that person.

- Friendships will differentiate into general and special friendships.

Ten to twelve years: preparing for adolescence

- Puberty is likely to have started. Their bodies begin to change due to the higher production of sex hormones at this age. This has an impact on their mental development, their emotions and their feelings towards another or same sex.

Summary

This chapter has provided an overview of some of the key theories and research that help us understand how children develop socially, relationally and emotionally and the conditions they need in order to develop healthy relationships. In the next chapters, we will focus more specifically on different age groups, sexual development and ways that you can help children learn about relationships and sexuality.

Chapter 5

Supporting Children's Development and Learning in Relationships and Sexuality

Birth to Three Years

Introduction

The focus of this and the following three chapters is on the 'how and what?', or the practicalities, of teaching children about the various aspects of sexuality and relationships. These chapters aim to answer many of the questions that parents, carers and professionals told us they needed help with when we did our research for this book. We outline which topics can be addressed at each stage of development and we suggest how you can communicate about these topics.

Our guidance is based on several excellent international guidelines and standards, namely:

- *Standards for Sexuality Education in Europe* by the World Health Organization's Regional Office for Europe and BZgA[1] (Sanderijn is a member of the expert group).

- UNESCO's *International Technical Guidance on Sexuality Education.*[2]

- The Sexuality Information and Education Council of the United States' *Guidelines for Comprehensive Sexuality Education.*[3]

- The Government of Western Australia's *Talk soon. Talk often* guidance.[4]

From all of these guidelines and standards, we have selected themes and topics that we consider important for children to learn about at specific ages:

- birth to three years

- four to six years

- seven to nine years

- ten to eleven years.

Each chapter deals with the needs of each age group separately, but please remember that age is only a guide when considering children's development. We realize that sometimes topics discussed in one chapter will appear in subsequent chapters, but this is necessary as the nature of the explanations need to change according to the child's age and stage of development.

The guidelines and standards we have listed give an excellent overview of the necessary themes and topics, but they often lack advice on how to address the topics in practice; this is what we want to offer you in these chapters. We will give lots of examples and suggest certain words so that you can implement the international guidance, but remember, these are just suggestions and you are free to use whatever words work best for you and your particular context.

Chapters 5–8 have a similar structure. We begin with the themes identified in the international guidelines and standards and, in tables, we outline the topics we consider important to address with the specific age group and we signpost you to the corresponding part of the chapter. We then discuss how to communicate about these topics with children, using the questions that were asked by parents, carers and professionals when we conducted our research for this book. We end each chapter with some suggestions for exercises or games to help make the learning process fun.

Relationships and sexuality education from birth to three years

Topics	Questions and answers
The human body and human development	
Names of all parts of the body and their functions	Questions 1, 2 and 3 and Exercise 1
Different bodies and different sexes	Question 3
Names of male and female genitals (and knowing how they can vary)	Questions 1, 2 and 3
Promoting positive body image and self-image: self-esteem	Questions 1, 2 and 3

Fertility and reproduction	
Pregnancy, birth and babies	Question 4
Basics of human reproduction (where babies come from)	Question 4
Sexuality	
Enjoyment of physical closeness is a normal part of everyone's life	Question 5
Tenderness and physical closeness as an expression of love and affection	Question 5
Enjoyment and pleasure when touching one's own body and genitals	Questions 6 and 7
Discovery of own body and own genitals	Questions 6 and 7
Gaining awareness of gender identity and equality	Question 8
Ability to talk about what feels nice and what doesn't feel nice physically	Questions 6 and 9
Ability to express own needs, wishes and boundaries	Question 10
Emotions	
Positive feelings towards their own sex and gender	Questions 1, 2 and 3
Awareness of 'yes' and 'no' feelings and how to express them	Exercise 2 and Question 9
Express and communicate own wishes and needs	Exercise 2 and Question 9

Relationships and lifestyles	
Different family relationships	Question 10
Sexuality, health and well-being	
Appreciation of their own body	Questions 1, 2, 5 and 6
Sexuality and rights	
The right to be curious about their own body	Question 6
The right to explore gender identities	Question 8
The right to ask questions about sexuality	Questions 1, 2, 3 4 and 10
The right to be safe and protected	Exercise 2
The responsibility of adults for the safety of children	Exercise 2
Social and cultural determinants of sexuality	
Social rules and cultural norms and values related to relationships and sexuality	Questions 6, 8 and 10
Differentiate between private and public behaviour	Questions 6 and 9
Acceptance of social rules about privacy and intimacy	Questions 6 and 9
Respect for social rules and cultural norms	Questions 6 and 7
Behave appropriately according to context	Questions 6, 7 and 9
Respect for their own and others' bodies	Question 9
Respect for 'no' or 'yes' from others	Question 10 and Exercise 2

Question 1: 'How can I talk with a baby about various parts of the body?'

Although babies can't yet talk, they learn about language from your words and non-verbal expressions. Using words when you interact with a baby not only contributes to their language development, but it is also an opportunity to bond. There are lots of different opportunities to name the parts of the body throughout a routine day, for example when dressing, bathing and playing. By giving a name to every part of the body, including the genitals, the baby will learn that each part is important, because it has a name.

Take a look at the example here where a parent or carer is bathing a baby or a child:

'Let me wash your head and face. Where is your nose and where are your eyes? Now let me wash your belly and now your arms. Where are your elbows and where are your armpits? Okay, and now we wash your back and your bottom/bum/buttocks. Where's your bottom/bum/buttocks? Let's not forget to wash your penis/vulva (or any other name you want to give). And now your legs, knees and ankles. And finally, your feet and toes (tickling the bottom of their feet).'

Exercise 1, at the end of this chapter, is a great way of helping two- and three-year-olds learn the different names of the various parts of the body.

Question 2: 'What should I call the genitals?'

Avoiding using a name for the genitals and just pointing or

saying 'down below' is still common for some, but this makes communicating about this part of the body difficult for children. In addition, if something has no name this might imply that it is unimportant or even unmentionable. Some experts argue that adults should teach children the correct terms for the genitals from a young age, for example 'penis' and 'vulva', but we don't think it matters what name you use, as long as you, as the parent or carer, feel comfortable with the word and that you choose a word that is likely to be understood by other adults who care for your child. However, you will need to explain that people use many different words for the genitals, and penis and vulva are the formal names. A point to mention here is that the term 'vagina' is often used incorrectly, instead of 'vulva'. The vulva is the external part of the female genitalia, including the labia, urethra, external part of the clitoris and vaginal opening. The vagina is the channel inside the vulva to the cervix.

Here's an example of how to introduce these words from an early age:

Carer when changing a child's nappy: 'Oh, you've pooped a lot! What a big child you are. Let me clean your bottom/ buttocks and your penis/vulva. That's better, here's a new nappy.'

Question 3: 'How can I explain the difference between bodies?'

Communicating with under threes about their body and others' bodies is an easy, natural topic for children. They can be very curious to know all about these things, which can make communication very easy and relaxed if you respond simply.

By talking to young children openly, at their level, they soon learn appropriate language and they also learn that talking about the body, including intimate parts, is normal and even fun to do. Here's an example:

Carer with three-year-old girl during bathing or changing clothes: 'Do you know what this part of the body is called (pointing at the bottom/buttocks/bum or whatever else you call it)?'

Child (laughing): 'Bum!'

Carer: 'Great! Yes! And what's the bum for?'

Child: 'To sit on.'

Carer: 'Yes, good, and what else?'

Child: 'To pooooop…!' (Child and carer both start to laugh.)

Carer (pointing at the part between the legs): 'And this, what is this called?'

Child (laughing again): 'Peepee, or something? I don't know, what is it called?'

Carer: 'There are many different names like vulva, or foo foo, or rosebud, or… What do you want to call it?'

Child: 'Peepee. Do you have a peepee as well?'

Carer: 'Yes, I have one too. But I call it my vulva. That is the same as peepee. People have different words for it. You can call it what you like. And do you know what a vulva or peepee is for?'

Child: 'To pee?'

Carer: 'True, but the peepee or vulva is also for delivering a baby when you are grown-up. Your pee comes out of a small opening and a baby from another opening. Both openings can be found in the vulva.'

Child: 'And what about my daddy? Does he have a peepee?'

Carer: 'Your daddy has no vulva but has a penis. Some people call it different things, like willy or dinky or... I prefer the word penis so that's what I call it.'

Child: 'Can I see a penis?'

Carer: 'People might not feel comfortable showing their penis to others. A penis and a vulva are parts of the body which are not shown in public to everyone. At home, people can choose whether they want to be naked or not. If you want to see a penis, I can show you a picture in our children's book about bodies. Do you know what a penis is for?'

Child: 'To deliver babies too?'

Carer: 'No, people with a penis can't carry and deliver babies. But they can help to make a baby. Do you know any other differences in bodies?

Child (points to the carer's breasts): 'Yes, these!'

Carer: 'Great, yes, some people get breasts when they grow older. But when other people get older they will not get breasts. Some people will get lots of hair on their chest and on their legs and on their face, like your daddy.'

Question 4: 'Can I have babies too?'

Questions about babies are the most frequently asked questions from children at this age; often they are also the most feared questions by adults! But when a young child asks this kind of question, you don't need to provide a detailed explanation about reproduction because this isn't what the child is asking. They just want to know if they can have a baby too, now or later in life. Or they might just want to know where the baby comes out of when they are born.

On behalf of young children all over the world, we ask you to avoid lengthy explanations! Our experience of more than 30 years in sexuality education is that young children under four years old are not interested in the origins of a baby. This is not how young children think. They just accept that a baby is there but when they see a mother's belly growing they might wonder: *How does it get out?* Some may think a baby will be pooped out, or that it comes out of the navel, or out of the mother's mouth if she vomits. And even if a smart child knows that the baby comes out of the opening between the mother's legs, called the vagina, they often can't imagine that the opening is big enough. So, when a young child asks, 'Can I have babies too?', don't panic, just remember to keep your response short and simple. You might want to use this type of response:

Child: 'Can I have babies too?'

Adult: 'Yes, when you are grown up, if you want to and if you are lucky you will be able to have babies too. Girls become women and women (you can also say: some people) have room in their belly where a baby can grow until it is big enough to come out. Boys become men and men (you can also say: other people) don't have room in their belly for a baby to grow but they can help make a baby. Do you know where the baby comes out of when it's ready?'

Child: 'Out of the bum when the mummy has to poop?'

Adult: 'No, only poop comes out of the bum. A baby can come out of the mummy's belly by moving down through a channel in the lower part of the belly. That channel is called the vagina and it ends in an opening between the legs. Most babies come out of the vagina.'

Child: 'Okay, I want a baby too when I am grown up. When are we having dinner?'

Question 5: 'Is baby massage a good idea?'

We know, from lots of research, that skin touch is essential in the development of a young baby. The need for skin touch continues in many children as they grow older, and even adults can feel the need to be touched, hugged and to have physical closeness. Touching a newborn's skin increases their weight and height, has a soothing and calming effect on restless babies, decreases their level of stress hormone cortisol and increases the well-being hormone serotonin.[5] Babies need their skin to be touched, caressed or massaged by their parents and carers to increase their well-being and to feel safe and happy. When gentle caressing or massage is accompanied by soft music or singing voices, the baby learns that this environment, these actions and these carers are making them safe and happy. This provides a solid foundation for positive and healthy social development. So yes, skin-to-skin massage is certainly a good idea!

Question 6: 'Is it normal for babies and toddlers to touch their genitals?'

Children generally start to touch their genitals at around four to six months. Babies enjoy the feelings that they experience when they happen to touch their genitals but up until the age of about one the baby immediately forgets what causes this nice feeling. Around their first birthday, which coincides with memory development, babies start to remember what causes this nice feeling and from that age onwards children start to touch their genitals deliberately again and again. They often go on to invent new ways of making this feeling happen, by using objects or by moving the body in different ways to stimulate the genitals. Boys know that these nice feelings come from the penis when they experience these sensations. But girls usually only know that the nice feelings come from a place between their legs and they are unaware that it is the vulva and the external part of their clitoris that gives them these feelings because they are more difficult for them to see.

The best response is to ignore this behaviour because it is harmless and can be comforting for the baby or young child. But for some adults this is difficult because they may spontaneously feel shock or disgust, depending on their own personal values, beliefs and upbringing. Try, if you can, to remember that this behaviour is a normal part of a child's sexual development. When parents or carers forbid or punish this behaviour, the message is clear to their child: these sensations are wrong or dirty, they should feel ashamed and they should not touch this part of their body because you will become angry with them. If this message is given frequently, the child will learn that anything that is related to sexuality and sexual feelings is wrong, dirty and shameful. And, we can assure you from our work that many adults' sexual problems can be related to these negative messages in their childhood. So, try to withhold any shock and disgust, count to ten, think back to what we have explained here and ignore the behaviour. For children who are aged three it may be helpful to explain some simple rules – for example: 'It's okay when you do this, but sometimes other people might not like to see you doing it'; 'So if you want to touch your... (name of the genital), it's better to do it in your bed or in your own room or at least somewhere where you do not bother other people'; 'Don't hurt yourself when doing it. It should be a nice feeling, not an unpleasant one.'

Question 7: 'Is it normal for young boys to have an erection?'

Little boys may have an erection in response to them touching their own genitals but it is usual for baby boys to have erections too. We know from ultrasound pictures that some baby boys have erections in the womb before they are born and many will have spontaneous erections several times a day and night from birth. These erections are not necessarily linked with sexual feelings but may occur because of fear, anxiety, stress, excitement or they may just be prompted by a subtle breeze tickling their penis when the nappy is being changed. The best response is to ignore the baby's erection and the same applies as he grows older.

It is worth noting, though, that some toddler boys can become upset by their erection as it might surprise them, feel strange or sometimes it might be a bit painful. In the first two instances the child will just need comforting and reassurance but if it feels painful at this age, it may be because the foreskin is still adhered to the skin on the top of the penis (the glans). This is normal for every non-circumcised boy and usually when a boy is six years old his foreskin will have separated from the skin of the glans and all these involuntary erections will make this process of separation easier. Sometimes this process takes until a boy is 11 years old. Never try to force your child's foreskin back before it's ready because it may be painful and damage the foreskin. If your son continues to be uncomfortable, it would be wise to make a visit to your family doctor.

Question 8: 'Is it okay for little boys to dress like a girl and vice versa?'

In Chapter 4, we explained how adults can subtly and unconsciously influence the development of a child's awareness of their gender, gender expression and gender role. By the time children are three years old they are usually aware of their gender and they are becoming increasingly conscious of how they feel they need to behave to gain approval or acceptance.

In Sweden, an experiment is currently taking place across several kindergartens where all references to gender have been removed. This means that children wear the same neutral clothes and are referred to in a gender-neutral term rather than 'he' or 'she' or 'him' or 'her'. The aim is that the children can develop behaviour, knowledge and skills which are independent from gender. We will not know the longer-term outcomes for several years, but short-term changes suggest that many children have demonstrated a reduced tendency to be influenced by gender stereotypes, compared to a control group of children from a typical Swedish pre-school.[6]

If you want to give children more opportunities to develop themselves beyond the usual norms of gender roles you could use several principles of the Swedish gender-neutral kindergartens. For example, you could encourage children to play with different kinds of toys, read books to them in which you change the original stereotypical names (the male hero in the story could be given a female name or the female in the book could become a boy), and you could encourage young children to wear any kind of clothes in which they feel comfortable, which includes little boys wearing dresses and little girls wearing superhero outfits! A book on gender that we would recommend for this age is

Who Are You? The Kid's Guide to Gender Identity by Brook Pessin Whedbee (published by Jessica Kingsley Publishers, 2016).

Sometimes parents are afraid that if their son wants to wear dresses at this age and if girls want to wear stereotypically masculine clothes they will become gay or lesbian. Being gay or lesbian is not caused by wearing particular clothes or playing with certain types of toys. A child's sexual orientation will develop regardless of the environment and cannot be changed by inhibiting or promoting certain behaviours or preferences. Gender identity and sexual orientation should not be confused.

Question 9: 'Should children be allowed to play "doctor games"?'

When children discover their own genitals and the nice feelings they get when touching them, they often become curious to see and touch other children's genitals. Playing doctors with friends of the same age becomes a very popular game for children between two and six years of age (and often even older). Undressing another child and examining their body and genitals is extremely exciting and is a normal part of sexual development when children reach around three years. But we understand that some parents, carers and professionals may feel uncomfortable with this kind of play and there is no problem with not allowing children to play these games, but it is important that you do not condemn this kind of play or tell the children off for playing in this way.

If you are happy for children to play doctors, they need some rules. This is what children should know (an example of a dialogue between a parent and a child about these rules can be found in the next chapter):

○ Always ask first.

○ Never force another child to join in or continue.

○ If the other child doesn't want to continue, you should stop.

○ Never insert an object into any opening of the body because that could hurt or injure the body.

○ If you don't want to join in or continue or if you just feel uncomfortable, say stop, walk away or find help.

○ You should only play this game with children of your own age.

This last point is worth emphasizing as differences in age may mean that an older child may persuade the younger child to go along with the game even if they are not comfortable to do so. Any other rules which you feel are important should also be clearly explained, such as which clothes (if any) must stay on and where the game should and shouldn't be played.

Question 10: 'How do I talk with my child about diversity and different kinds of families?'

Young children do not wonder what other children's families are like. Usually they assume that everyone's family is like their own and, if not, children at this age just accept a different constellation. To help children grow up with an open mind, it is important that they understand from an early age that children can grow up in different environments. When you read books or watch television together, if a child in the story comes from a traditional family, you could explain that not every child lives in that type of family. You could also use books which discuss diverse families, for example Todd Parr's *The Family Book* (published by Hachette Book Group, 2010). Normalizing diversity in families from a young age makes it easier for children to accept a situation that is different to their own. In the same way, you can talk about how people can feel love for anyone, regardless of whether they are a man or a woman. By doing this, you will begin to normalize more difficult (and sometimes stigmatizing) terms such as 'gay', 'lesbian' and 'bisexual'. Later, when your child grows older and comes across these terms, you will have already laid the foundations to explain these concepts further.

EXERCISE 1: LEARNING THE NAMES OF DIFFERENT PARTS OF THE BODY

This is a great exercise to do with children aged two to three years old.

Using a big piece of paper, ask your child to lie down on the paper and draw round the outline of their body with a marker pen. Once you've finished, sit together and ask what the names of the different parts of the body are. Depending on the age of the child, you can use more or less complicated names, like thigh, calf and ankle or, more simply, leg. Don't forget to name the genitals and explain the formal name (penis and vulva) and choose the name you will use in your house. If your child wants to, they could colour in where the names of the parts of the body belong or give the body some coloured clothes. Write your child's name at the bottom and hang it on the wall. Sometimes children will also want to play this game with you lying on the paper and they will draw a line around your body. This is a great opportunity to explain the differences between adults' and children's bodies.

EXERCISE 2: PRACTISING SAYING YES AND SAYING NO

Help your child to learn that clearly saying YES or NO is both allowed and important by doing some role play.

Ask your child the following questions and encourage them to respond as clearly as possible by using the word YES or NO and changing their body and voice to emphasize their response:

1. When your best friend wants to tickle you, how do you say YES or NO?

2. If an adult in the supermarket wants to tickle you, is that a YES or a NO for you? Show me how you would say this.

3. Someone in your class (use a name) wants you to play at his house. Is this a YES or a NO for you?

4. Someone with a big scary dog wants you to pet his dog.

Is this a YES or a NO for you? How does your scary NO sounds? Is it clear enough?

5. Your classmate wants to give you a kiss on the cheek. Is this a YES or a NO for you?

6. And if I want to give you a big kiss on your cheek, YES or NO?

You can add more questions, if you and your child like this game.

Chapter 6

Supporting Children's Development and Learning in Relationships and Sexuality

Four to Six Years

Introduction

As we outlined in Chapter 5, this chapter is concerned with the practical side of relationships and sexuality education and is based on international standards and guidelines (for the full explanation please refer to Chapter 5's Introduction). However, this time, the focus is on supporting children aged four to six years. We begin the chapter with an overview of the themes and topics identified from the international guidance and we then provide a discussion in a question and answer format, based on the questions posed by parents, carers and professionals when we asked them what they wanted from this book. To get the most out of this chapter, you can alter our suggestions to make them appropriate for your particular context.

Relationships and sexuality education for four- to six-year-olds

Topics	Questions and answers
The human body and human development	
Skin hunger	Question 1
Self-esteem	Question 2
Being happy with their own body	Question 3
Personal hygiene	Question 4
Fertility and reproduction	
Pregnancy, birth and dispelling myths	Question 5
Some people have babies, others don't	Question 6
Sexuality	
Enjoyment and pleasure when touching one's body	Question 7
Names of genitals	Questions 4 and 8
Sexual feelings: closeness, enjoyment, excitement as part of all human feelings	Questions 9, 10, 11 and 12
Respect for others' bodies (consent)	Questions 1, 11 and 12

Emotions	
Feelings of friendship and love	Questions 13, 14 and Exercise 2
Empathy	Question 15
Jealousy, anger and disappointment and how to deal with these emotions	Question 15
Relationships and lifestyles	
Diversity in relationships	Question 16
Respect for diversity	Questions 5, 6 and 16
Sexuality, health and well-being	
Ability to say yes/no	Questions 1 and 17
Awareness of own boundaries	Questions 1 and 17
Adults are responsible for the safety of the child	Question 17
Sexuality and rights	
Some people are not good	Question 17 and Exercise 1
Social and cultural determinants of sexuality	
Values and norms can differ by situation, country and culture	Questions 7 and 18
Promoting an open and non-judgemental attitude	Question 18
Gender equality	Question 19

Question 1: 'Can I still hug and touch a child at this age and what if they want to touch me?'

Skin touch remains important and shouldn't be stopped just because of the gender or age of the child; it should be continued as long as the child asks for it, wants it and allows it. This last point is important, because at this stage children are beginning to develop boundaries and it is essential that adults show respect for them. Breaking a child's boundaries repeatedly can have negative consequences, because the child will learn that boundaries don't matter and they may, therefore, be reluctant to both assert their own boundaries and respect others' boundaries as they grow up.

Respecting a young child's boundaries can be a real challenge for adults both emotionally and practically. If a child doesn't want to sit on your lap, it doesn't mean that they don't want to be consoled or read a book with you. Neither does it mean that they won't want to be hugged like a little baby the next time they feel lonely, sad, insecure or jealous of the attention their baby sister is getting! Young children don't have the vocabulary to express these complicated emotions, so it is best to follow their lead and respect what they want at that point in time. The same applies when your offer of help to dry your child off after a shower is refused. Even if you are in a hurry, respect their boundaries but try to solve the situation by giving a timeframe, for example: 'It's okay to dry yourself, but we are in a hurry, so be ready in two minutes please.'

Boundaries can also be expressed and taught by you as a parent or carer. Sometimes children like to see or touch their parents or carers' breasts or genitals. If you don't appreciate this, be clear with the child that you don't like being touched there. Just keep the message simple and short and the child will understand that people (including them) are allowed to refuse touch if they don't want it.

Question 2: 'Why is self-esteem important for healthy relationships and sexual development?'

Self-esteem is an essential ingredient for healthy relational and sexual development because children with low self-esteem can be more vulnerable to sexual abuse and they tend to be influenced by others more easily than children who are confident, emotionally balanced and satisfied with their bodies, their abilities and their self-worth.[1]

Self-esteem is a personality trait but it can be influenced positively or negatively by the child's environment. Children who are frequently judged, blamed or punished by their caregivers have a hard time thinking about themselves positively. Similarly, children with parents who have extremely high expectations can perceive themselves as failures if they can't reach these expectations.[2] Research shows that children who grow up in warm, open families where parents are open to listening to their children's opinions from an early age are more likely to be armed with confidence than children who don't.[3]

By the time they are four, most children will have built the foundations of their self-esteem. Practical strategies that contribute to a positive self-image include making positive remarks about their body and never calling children derogatory nicknames. Compliments about their behaviour and their efforts are more effective at raising self-esteem than those which praise the child or an outcome.[4] So, comments from parents, carers and teachers like: 'Wow, you've worked really hard on that drawing' or, 'Thank you for being such a great help' go a long way in enhancing a child's self-esteem.

Question 3: 'How important is it to teach children to be happy with their own bodies?'

Children aged four to six need to learn that their body is something precious that should be taken care of. At this age, children can learn to love their body with the help of caring adults. This is an integral part of their developing self-esteem and is, therefore, important to the development of positive relationships and sexuality. Children of this age may begin to notice that they are different from their peers and may become dissatisfied with how they look. This may be particularly relevant for children who have a particular physical challenge or disability as they may notice for the first time that they are different to other children. When children understand that although their body might look different to others, it doesn't make them less valuable. This can be a positive step towards becoming satisfied with their body.

Question 4: 'Should children at this age learn to clean their own genitals?'

Parents can help children at this age to clean their bodies and explain the importance of cleaning and taking care of their genitals. When doing this, you could use the proper names for the genitals and explain that in addition to family names there are also formal names (penis and vulva), which you can use increasingly now to familiarize your children with these words.

You can teach your child that when he takes a bath or a shower, he needs to wash the outside of his penis with luke-warm water (without soap). If he is not circumcised, teach him to gently pull his foreskin back a little bit in order for him to clean the top of his penis with some lukewarm water (again, no soap). If pulling back the foreskin is painful, he shouldn't pull it back quite so far, and he should stop before he feels any pain. It takes time for the foreskin to become flexible so if this is difficult for your child to do, don't worry as the skin will loosen as he matures.

Children can also learn to clean their own vulva for them-selves at this age, using lukewarm water. You can explain to your child that she can do this by splashing lukewarm water between her vulva lips. Again, it is advisable not to use soap.

Question 5: 'What should I say when children ask, "Where do babies come from?"'

Children at this age can be very interested in bodies in general; their own, their friends' and adults'. They are often fascinated by pregnancy and birth and ask lots of questions like: 'How is a baby born?' and 'Where do babies come from?' Questions like these are completely appropriate for children at this age because they are interested in understanding more about the complex world they are living in.

As we discussed in Chapter 2, children have the right to accurate answers to their questions, so even if you have to count up to ten or look the answer up, make sure that you answer simply and accurately. Don't tell them any myths as this can be very confusing for children and they may sense that you are reluctant to talk to them about relationships and sexuality, which may serve as a barrier to them asking you questions in the future.

Remember, just keep your answers short and simple. When children ask: 'Where do babies come from?' they just want an answer such as: 'A baby comes from the mummy's belly.' If they want to know how the baby comes out, they will ask and you can continue with the next short and simple answer, such as: 'Most babies come out of their mummy's vagina. Remember that is the opening between a woman's legs?' For most children at this stage this is enough; they will be satisfied and continue with their play. If not, they might ask a further question, like: 'Was I born like that?' If you are the child's parent you might respond: 'Yes, you were born like that' or 'No, some children are born differently. A doctor opens up the mummy's belly and takes the baby out and then closes her belly again. That's how you were born' or 'You didn't come out of my body, but you came out of your other mother's body through her vagina (or through her belly with the help of a doctor).' If you are a teacher or carer you can simply say that you are not sure but give a general answer about the different ways babies are born.

If children at this age have more questions like: 'Is it painful?' or 'Can I have babies too?' you can give the same style of answer outlined above. For this age group, a simple response is enough but of course, any parent or carer who wishes to provide more detail is free to do so. Here is a suggestion of an explanation that you could adapt to help you explain where a baby comes from:

A baby can be made when a sperm from a man meets the egg cell of a woman in her belly. When a man and a woman make love together, they have sex. The man puts his penis in the woman's vagina. This is what adults sometimes do when they love each other. When sperm from the penis comes into the vagina, it can swim to the woman's belly. There the sperm might meet an egg cell. Or a doctor can help put a sperm and egg together and put it into the woman's belly. When the sperm and egg meet each other, they might join together and slowly grow into a baby. The baby is very small at first, like a little dot. But it will grow in the mother's belly until it is big enough to come out. You can see from the outside that her belly becomes bigger and bigger until the baby is ready to be born. Most babies are born through the vagina. Others will come out of the belly when the doctor makes an opening in the mother's belly. There are also children who came from one mother but live in another family. Their first mother loved them very much but was not able to take care of them. That's why some children grow up in another family.

Question 6: 'I am a primary school teacher. A five-year-old asked me why I have no babies. How should I answer?'

The same principles that we outlined in Question 5 apply to this type of question. Here are some suggestions for you to adapt:

Child: 'Why don't you have children?'

Adult: 'Because I just want to wait a bit longer before starting to have children. I am too busy taking care of all of you to have my own baby.'

Or:

Adult: 'I have no children because I don't have a partner and I don't want to have a baby on my own. So, first I have to find a sweet partner who wants to have a child with me.'

Or:

Adult: 'I have no children because I don't want any. I love taking care of all of you and that is enough joy for me. Not all people want to have children.'

Or:

Adult: 'I would love to have a child, but it's not always easy to make a baby and although I have tried, I can't.'

Question 7: 'What should I do when my child masturbates?'

In the previous chapter, we explained that babies, toddlers and young children touch their own genitals because they like how it feels. We call this behaviour masturbation but it is important to emphasize that masturbation for adults serves different purposes to those for children. For many adults, masturbation is closely related to feeling sexually aroused and wanting to reach an orgasm to release (sexual) stress. This is not the case for young children. Most children at this age touch their genitals because they know it gives them a nice feeling and it makes them relaxed and, sometimes, sleepy. For children, this behaviour is not related in any sense to sexuality. From research[5] it is known that many children masturbate and some research[6] shows that although rare, some children can reach orgasm (although this will be without ejaculation in boys).

At this age, children are becoming increasingly aware of social rules because they are at kindergarten or pre-school or school and have had to learn how to behave in a group. In the same way that they learn to wait their turn to speak and that they cannot leave the classroom without the teacher's permission, they learn about rules for touching the genitals. Children quickly learn that this is inappropriate at school. For some children, these rules might be different from the rules at home, but this is okay. They are now learning that society has different rules for different contexts and they will also gradually begin to learn that there are rules related to intimacy, gender, body exposure and nudity.

If you notice that your child is masturbating and you feel that it is in an inappropriate place, you could say something like: 'I know it feels good when you do that, but remember I told you other people might not like to see it. So, it's better to do this somewhere where you won't bother others. Okay?' By saying it in this way, you convey the message that the behaviour is not wrong, but the context is inappropriate.

Question 8: 'What words should we use for the genitals at this stage?'

Intimate family names are not enough now as children may need to use more exact language at this age to explain themselves, so they also need to be familiar with more formal words like penis or vulva. Being familiar with these terms also enables children to understand what adults mean. Examples might include a doctor explaining that she needs to examine the child's penis or vulva or an adult with bad intentions who says the same thing. If they don't know these words, children will be unable to say 'No' if they feel uncomfortable. Or they might say 'Yes' because they think *It's okay as long as that person doesn't touch my peepee.* If you find these words too difficult, too clinical or too vulgar for children at this age, you can still use the family terms but at least tell your child that these formal terms exist.

For both boys and girls, it is important that they also learn that their genitals comprise different parts so that they can begin to learn about their bodies. The parts of the penis are the shaft and the glans. On the top of the glans is the urethra (or the pee-hole). The glans is the most sensitive part of the penis. The vulva consists of the vulva lips (labia), two on the outside and two on the inside, the urethra (pee-hole), the clitoris (of which only a small bump is visible, with the bigger part inside the body) and the vaginal opening at the bottom of the vulva.

The small bump of the clitoris can be very sensitive when touched, as can the rest of the vulva. These kinds of details can be readily explained to most children in this age group but if you feel uncomfortable doing this, at least explain one or two parts of the penis and vulva and give some further information when they are a year or two older.

Question 9: 'Do children experience sexual feelings at this age?'

The pleasurable feelings that children experience when they touch their genitals (or when touching or looking at other children's genitals while playing doctor-type games) can be called sexual feelings and continue at this stage, even when parents or carers have been very strict or negative about it. It's a natural feeling in humans, regardless of age or gender. Awareness of these feelings and how to provoke them becomes clearer at this stage and some children want to experience these feelings more frequently. Although they are learning social rules now, the urge to experience these feelings can overrule the knowledge that it might be inappropriate.

Question 10: 'What should I do if my child accidently walks in on us having sex?'

If a child walks in on you having sex and they ask you what you were both doing, you can answer the question in the way suggested here:

Child: 'What were you both doing?'

Parent: 'We were making love. That's what adults do when they love each other. It means we are happy and we feel nice.'

Child: 'Oh…can I join in? I love you too!'

Parent: 'No, this is something only adults do together. If we want to show our love for you, we hug and cuddle and kiss you. Shall we do that now?'

Child: 'Yes, I want a big hug now. From both of you!'

Question 11: 'I walked in on my four-year-old son licking his friend's penis. I am so worried; he must have copied this behaviour from someone else – surely he wouldn't just think of it on his own?'

This question may seem shocking but it is not unusual. Internationally we have seen newspaper headlines describing four year olds in this context as perpetrators and victims of sexual abuse. However, this kind of language is entirely inappropriate and can be stigmatizing and potentially damaging to a child's development.

At this age, children can be so curious to see and touch others' bodies that they can do things to satisfy their curiosity that might surprise us as adults. Licking genitals can be one of these behaviours. They have just left behind the developmental stage in which they have tried to research every new object by putting it in their mouths. Children up to the age of four or five often still do this. So, licking a friend's penis (or a girl's vulva) could be a spontaneous action to research a new part of the body as part of a 'doctor game'. If this is the situation, it doesn't mean that the behaviour is age-appropriate though and children need to learn that this kind of game is not allowed. As a parent or educator, you can be very clear and strict about this rule. You want them to understand and obey you. You can give them an alternative, like playing doctors in another way or perhaps just offer them a totally different game to distract them, like doing a puzzle or playing outside.

However, you also need to be sure that this behaviour was not copied from a picture, a video or observed behaviour by an older sibling or an adult. To explore this, you should have a serious talk with your child, asking why he wanted to lick his friend's penis, whether he has ever seen anyone else doing this and whether anyone has ever asked him to do this to them. This kind of conversation needs to be handled very carefully, so that the child doesn't feel frightened, blamed or judged because if he does, he will deny everything and close down.

Needless to say, if a child says that he has copied this behaviour or someone has done it to him, you need to seek professional support. We have provided resources that you may find useful at the end of this book but your family doctor will also be able to help you.

Question 12: 'How can I teach my child about consent?'

You can readily discuss the concept of consent (mutual permission) with a child by using examples from their everyday lives. For example, one mother told us how she had taught her four-year-old son about consent by encouraging him to ask his special friend if he was happy for him to hold his hand in the playground, as the friend had previously been upset when he had just grabbed it. So, his mum talked to him about checking first and respecting his friend's choice and allowing the friend to change his mind if he had said yes but no longer wanted to. Through using a situation that was meaningful to her son, the mother introduced him to the fundamental aspects of consent.

You can do this in the context of other aspects of play because when two or more children are playing together, consent is a very important condition to have so that all partners in the game participate happily. This is an important rule in every playful interaction, but it is especially the case when children play games related to sexuality, such as a doctor game. In these kinds of games, children will experience sexual feelings (although they won't recognize them as such – they will just recognize these feelings as pleasurable) and if there is no clear consent, these feelings could be associated with force, threat, intimidation, power or even pain. In addition, if consent is not upheld, children may learn that their boundaries or personal limits can be violated by others or that it doesn't make sense to object to something you don't want because it will happen anyway. Alternatively, they may learn that by pushing someone else's boundaries, through force or intimidation, you can get what you want.

Games that involve some level of intimacy should always be accompanied by several rules:

○ Always ask first.

○ Never force another child to join in or continue.

○ If the other child doesn't want to continue, you should stop.

○ Never insert an object into any opening of the body because that could hurt or injure the other child's or your body.

○ If you don't want to join in or continue, or if you just feel uncomfortable, say stop, walk away or find help.

○ You should only play this game with children of your own age.

If you need some kind of framework for yourself in judging whether play is consensual, you might find the following principles helpful:

○ There should be no more than three years' age difference between the children.

○ There should be no significant power difference between the children, for example: height, weight, character and number.

○ There should be an opportunity for all children to say no at any time.

You can read more about this in Chapter 9.

Here's an example of a casual conversation that illustrates these points:

Parent: 'What are you doing?'

Child: 'I am playing doctors with Danny.'

Parent: 'Did you ask Danny if he wants to play that game?'

Child: 'Yes, I did and I want to play it too.'

Parent: 'Okay, and you both still know the rules we have agreed for this game?'

Child: 'Don't put objects inside openings, right? And when I don't like it any more, I should say stop, right?'

Parent: 'Great! And if Danny doesn't like it and he tells you, you should do what?'

Child: 'Stop as well, I think?'

Parent: 'Yes, great! I will be ready with the milk and cookies in a moment. Come down when I call you. Okay?'

Question 13: 'How can I help children understand what makes a good friendship?'

Children at this stage are able to develop friendships and they will learn and experience a lot about what works and what doesn't work in social relationships. This is extremely valuable because all the principles they learn about friendships and relationships will be used by them later when they are ready to form romantic relationships. However, they still need support with developing friendships and in learning which values are important in a friendship. Make a list for yourself outlining what you think is important in a good and healthy friendship and general relationships, and what you want your child to learn. See the exercise at the end of this chapter about how you can help your child make good friendships.

Question 14: 'My five-year-old says he wants to marry his best friend. What should I say?'

Children at this stage of development can differentiate between different kinds of love and friendship feelings. Some can feel a deep feeling of love for their best friend and another type of love for their teacher or parent. However, they may still lack the necessary vocabulary to articulate all these different feelings. They will have heard the phrase 'falling or being in love' and some of them may use these words to express special friendship feelings for special friends. This can lead to children of this age group saying that they are in love with their best friend, their teacher, their mother/father or their dog. What they mean is that they are especially fond of or love these people and their pets. Here's an example of a conversation that may help you think through what you might say to a child who expresses similar emotions to those in this particular parent's question:

Child (boy): 'Dad, do you love mummy?'

Father: 'Yes, I love her very much. That's why we decided to live together and have you.'

Child: 'I love my best friend, Danny.'

Father: 'That's great son. To love someone is a great feeling.'

Child: 'I want to marry him when I grow up because we've decided to never leave each other.'

Father: 'Wow, wonderful! Has Danny told you that he loves you too?'

Child: 'Yes, but his dad says that this isn't real love. Only grown-ups can feel real love. And he says that we will both end up marrying a girlfriend. Is that true?'

Father: 'What you feel now is really true. This is real love for you. But we never know how long love will last, because we might change. Maybe you and Danny will still love each other in the future, maybe not. We will see, but it doesn't matter. For now, just enjoy your feelings for Danny.'

Question 15: 'How can we talk about emotions?'

The aim at this stage of development is to give children the language to express how they feel. Becoming aware of what they are feeling and being able to express and label their emotions is an important part of social-emotional development. As we discussed in Chapter 4, people with a highly developed social-emotional sense have better and more satisfying relationships because they are able to reflect on their own emotions, talk about them and manage them. They are also better at understanding others' emotions, which can lead to better relationships.

So, what can we do? As we explained in Chapter 4, you can start by verbally labelling the four basic emotions: happy, angry, afraid and sad. You can also ask your child if they can recognize your emotions. Make a habit of talking about their feelings whenever you notice they are showing one of the basic emotions. In this way, they will learn that thinking about what they feel and talking about it is good. Gradually, you can add in more complicated emotions whenever the child is showing them. For example, feeling 'sad' can have many different nuances, which can help a child better understand why they are feeling that specific way. Now you can also help your child to deal with strong negative emotions. By this stage, children are able to understand that when they feel angry towards another child, hitting or fighting is not the best way to address their feelings. By acknowledging their emotions, rather than playing them down, ignoring them or becoming angry because of their behaviour, you can show that you understand what they feel, label this feeling, check it with your child and finally, help them find a solution to solve the situation which evokes this negative feeling. This style of parenting is what psychologist John Gottman calls 'emotion coaching', as discussed in Chapter 1. Here's an example that you may find useful:

> Your oldest child, who is aged four, has been showing negative behaviours since the arrival of his newborn sister. You understand that he might be a bit jealous, so you have been patient with him. Every time you breastfeed the baby, your son starts to yell and scream, so with the baby in your arms you try to give him some attention. Suddenly he walks up to you and pushes the baby aside, saying: 'I want to sit on your lap.' Pushing the baby is beyond your limit and you explode angrily: 'Why did you do that? Your sister is just a tiny baby, she doesn't want to harm you.' But you manage to stop yourself going further by counting to ten and waiting for your emotions to calm down. Instead of sending him to his room, you say: 'Come here darling, sit with me and your sister.' With one arm you hold the baby and you use the other arm to cuddle your son. Gently (although you might be still fuming inside), you say: 'Tell me, why did you push your sister away?' He responds: 'Because I want to sit there, by you. The baby is always in your arms and I never am.' You respond: 'I can see you are angry, that's why you reacted in that way. Is that right?' Your son nods, he is still a bit angry but feels better because you are listening to him. You go on to say: 'Now, I can imagine it is sometimes difficult for you now that you have a baby sister and you

don't get as much attention from me and Daddy that you got before she was born. Is that right?' He nods again and lays his head on your lap. You stroke his face and then you say: 'Although I understand you're feeling angry, pushing your sister is not a nice thing to do. I don't want you to do that again. If you are angry with your sister or with me it's better to show it in another way. What would be a better way?' Your son thinks about this and says: 'Maybe I should walk away and yell to you that I want to sit on your lap?' You reply by saying something like this: 'That would be better but I think just telling me rather than yelling would be even better. Okay? And would it help if every time I breastfeed the baby, you come and sit close to me and we can watch the baby feeding and falling asleep together and then I could read a story with you. Would you like that?'

Question 16: 'How can we talk about different kinds of relationships and families?'

As children grow older and start to mix more widely at kindergarten and school, they learn that other children might have family structures that are different from theirs. Their perceptions of other family structures will be shaped by the values conveyed in their own environment. For example, if children hear comments like: 'It's sad that Jake lives alone with his mum' or 'Charlie's dad could do with a wife – men are no good at child rearing' or 'That girl in your class with the two mums will really miss having a father', they will quickly adopt these negative attitudes themselves.

Explaining to your child that not everyone needs to live in the same kind of family as yours will help them develop tolerant views regarding difference and diversity. Children can be quite traditional in their thinking at this stage because strict structures give them security and make the world feel less complex. By explaining that other kinds of relationships are just as good as the way your family lives, the child will be better placed to accept and respect other families and relationships which are different to their own.

Here's a brief example that may help you formulate your own explanations:

Child: 'Why are those two men walking hand in hand?'

Carer: 'Because they love each other. When people love each other, they sometimes want to touch each other tenderly, or they may want to kiss or hold hands.'

Child: 'What about two women?'

Carer: 'It's the same, they can also love each other and when they want to they can walk hand in hand or kiss or make love to each other.'

Child: 'Can they make a baby?'

Carer: 'If they want to, they can have a baby together. But they cannot make it together. For a baby, you need the sperm from a man and the egg from a woman to come together.'

Child: 'Okay, can I go to the playground now?'

Question 17: 'Will children at this age become anxious if we talk about risks?'

Sexuality education is not complete without mentioning the less positive sides of sexuality. The aim of comprehensive sexuality education is for children to become informed and empowered in an age-appropriate and developmentally appropriate way about this beautiful and natural part of their development and for them to feel comfortable with their own body, feelings and gender. But at the same time, they need to become aware that to stay happy, comfortable and safe, they need to follow some rules which can help them to avoid risks. Parents do not relinquish their responsibility by explaining these rules though and they should never blame the child for not following the rules if something negative happens.

Explaining risks doesn't mean that a child will become anxious but how and when you talk about these issues with children is important. This stage is perfect for starting these conversations. Here's some guidance:

- When your child has just turned four, introduce the general topic of listening to rules. You can explain that rules help people stay safe. Relatable examples could include stopping at red traffic lights, not hurting other people, looking both ways before crossing the road and so on. You could explain that obeying social rules is wise because it helps reduce the risk of getting hurt.

- Follow your explanation with a discussion about the importance of being clear in what you want and do not want and the importance of saying 'yes' or 'no'. As we said previously, children can only do this if they know what they want and don't want, and parents can help their children to develop this skill by giving them choices in what they eat, wear, who they play with and so on from a young age. This way, children become aware of what they really want or do not want because they are encouraged to reflect on their desires and aversions and they also learn that they have the right to express themselves. This is not always easy for four-year-old children, but by starting this learning process young, they will benefit a lot later in life. Although this may seem a long way off, this will help them when they need to make decisions related to their sexual life. Of course, a compromise needs to be reached in day-to-day chores that children might not enjoy like brushing their teeth, clearing the table or eating their vegetables, but the message is that if a child feels uncomfortable with a request, with the person who is making the request or with the specific situation, they should be clear in saying 'no'. If the requester doesn't stop their behaviour or persists with their request, the child should get away from the situation and seek help. And finally, tell your child to rely on you when they are feeling uncomfortable with an experience. Being able to trust that their parents will always be there to help, without any judgement, anger or blame, is pivotal to child-parent relationships.

- You can also introduce other people's boundaries at this stage by explaining that their friends will have their own boundaries, just like they have theirs, and boundaries need to be respected, by others but also by them.

Question 18: 'My ideas about nudity are different from other parents. How should I talk about this with my child?'

As we said earlier, when a child starts school or pre-school, their world expands and they begin to learn about different ways of living and different rules. This applies when they start to go on playdates at their friends' homes too. For example, they learn new rules about how to interact with adults, how to sit at a table drinking lemonade and even new rules about watching television. These experiences give children lots of new messages and support the development of an open mind, but they can be a challenge too. You can prepare your child for this by explaining that different families have different habits and that it is polite to adjust your normal habits as long as you don't go beyond your own limits.

In relation to nudity, here's an example of a conversation that you may find helpful:

Parent: 'You're going for your first sleepover tomorrow with your friend Tina. Are you looking forward to it?'

Child: 'Ohh yes, I am soooo excited!'

Parent: 'I am sure it will be great fun for both of you. But let me explain some things to you before you go. In our family, we have a bath before going to sleep, right? And after bathing you love to run through the house naked for a couple of minutes, right?'

Child: 'Yep.'

Parent: 'But I'm not sure if they do the same thing in Tina's family.'

Child: 'Ohh, why not? Shall I ask Tina to do it with me?'

Parent: 'It would be better to ask her mum first. And if she doesn't agree, it would be better and more polite for you to wait until you come home to run around naked. Okay?'

Child: 'Yes. But when Tina comes to my house for a sleepover, we can ask her to do it with me here, can't we?

Parent: 'Yes. But if she doesn't want to that's okay. You can just save the running game for another day. I want Tina to feel comfortable when she is in our house. I know she is not allowed to eat certain foods, so I will prepare food for her that she is comfortable eating. And if she doesn't want to take a shower or bath before sleeping, that's okay for me. Every family has different habits and it is important that we respect them.'

Question 19: 'Is gender equality relevant at this stage?'

The principles that we outline with regards to gender equality in Chapter 5 remain the same for this age group. At this stage, children's gender identity is often still fluid. They tend to have no issues with playing someone of another sex as part of a game because they know that outside the game they have another gender. At the same time, what we see at this age is that some children want to be seen and recognized as their biological sex. They observe older people to see how they behave and dress and they like to copy them. They are also influenced by the subtle messages that societies convey about gender, in relation to their capabilities and behavioural expectations. So, gender equality is highly relevant at this stage. For some additional perspectives, you may be interested in the BBC documentary, *No More Boys and Girls. Can Your Kids Go Gender-Free?*[‡] which illustrates differences in gender beliefs at this stage and how gender beliefs can be shaped to become healthier ones.

---

‡   www.youtube.com/watch?v=wN5R2LWhTrY

EXERCISE 1: THE 'WHAT WOULD YOU DO IF...?' GAME

To help your child think about how they would seek help in uncomfortable situations, you could play the following game, which most children love at this age!

Tell your child that you will ask questions and they need to give you the best answer they can. You can play this game anywhere and at any time – in the car, after dinner, walking back from school and so on. It can be done with one child or with a group of children. Every answer should be rewarded, even if you consider the response quite unrealistic:

- What would you do if you lost me in a very crowded shopping centre?

- What would you do if you're playing outside and a man or a woman offers you a sweet?

- What would you do if you're playing outside and someone in a car asks you to show them the way?

- What would you do if school has finished, but your usual carer is not there yet to pick you up and a strange man or woman offers to take you home?

- What would you do if you're in the swimming pool and a nice man you don't know wants you to go down the water slide with him?

- What would you do if you wanted to hug your friend?

- What would you do if one of your friends wanted to hug you?

EXERCISE 2: WHO IS YOUR FRIEND?

Sit with your child and think of an imaginary friend. Make a list of likes and dislikes about the friend by asking the child to complete the sentences below.

A good friend
should be:

I will be a good
friend when I:

. . . .

. . . .

. . . .

. . . .

. . . .

. . . .

A good friend
should not be:

I will not be a good
friend when I:

. . . .

. . . .

. . . .

. . . .

. . . .

. . . .

Chapter 7

Supporting Children's Development and Learning in Relationships and Sexuality

Seven to Nine Years

Introduction

Before reading this chapter, you may find it helpful to refer to the Chapter 5 Introduction which outlines our guidance for Chapters 5–8 as well as the international standards that underpin each of these chapters. In addition, before you dive in to this chapter, we want to just take a moment to return to something we discussed in the main introduction when we talked about a very important goal in sexuality education which is to help empower children in making their own healthy and responsible decisions related to relationships and sexuality.

As we outlined in the previous chapter, children aged between four and six years are not yet capable of making all of their own decisions. Parents have to help them, but they can also promote and stimulate the development of decision-making skills by giving them choices such as: 'What fruit do you want to take to school, apple or grapes?' or 'What do you want to do first before we have dinner, clear away your toys or lay the table?' In this way, children learn to think about what they want and don't want and they also start to think about the possible consequences of their choices. The latter is difficult for younger children, but between seven and nine years of age, children become increasingly able to consider the consequences of their choices. This is a very important skill for them to have as they mature and need to take decisions related to relationships and sexuality.

At seven to nine years, children need guiding in the development of this important skill, first by giving them opportunities for making day-to-day choices and, when they are ready, by involving them in family decisions, such as choosing a pet, moving to a new house or picking a holiday destination. If children feel involved in some adult decisions, they feel appreciated and taken seriously and, importantly, they begin to learn that every decision has consequences and that thinking ahead about possible implications can make for more balanced and informed decision-making.

This is a theme that we will return to throughout this chapter, but first, the chapter begins with the themes identified in the international guidelines and standards and, in tables, we outline the topics we consider important to address with seven- to nine-year-olds and we signpost you to the corresponding parts of the chapter. We then go on to discuss how to communicate about these topics with this age group, using a question and answer format along with some practical examples. We end the chapter with some suggestions for exercises or games that you can play with children to reinforce some of the themes that we highlight.

Relationships and sexuality education for seven- to nine-year-olds

Topics	Questions and answers
The human body and human development	
Positive gender identity	Question 1 and 6
Gender roles	Question 1
Self-esteem and gender	Questions 1 and 5
Acceptance and respect for other genders	Question 1
Biological differences between men and women (internal and external)	Question 2
Correct names for male and female genitals (and how they can vary)	Questions 2 and 3
Body changes, menstruation, ejaculation, individual variation	Question 3
Privacy	Question 4
Promoting positive body image and self-image: self-esteem	Question 5 and Exercise 1
Fertility and reproduction	
Different approaches to reproduction	Question 7
Introducing contraception	Question 7
Different forms of families	Question 8
Some people have children, others don't	Question 8
Marriage and other ways of living (together or single)	Question 8

Sexuality	
Dealing with images of love and the media	Question 13
Dealing with sex in the media	Questions 13 and 14
Awareness that sex can be pleasurable	Questions 12 and 15
Emotions	
Feelings of love	Questions 10 and 11 and Exercise 2
Relationships and lifestyles	
Friends and social relationships	Question 9
Communication skills and social relationships	Question 9
Sexuality, health and well-being	
Ability to express boundaries and consent	Question 16
Good and bad secrets	Question 17
Sexuality and rights	
The responsibility of adults for the safety of children	Questions 14, 17, 18, 19 and 20
Asking for help and information	Questions 17, 19 and 20
Abuse	Questions 19 and 20
Social and cultural determinants of sexuality	
Respect for different lifestyles, values and norms	Questions 8 and 12

Question 1: 'How can I prevent my child from conforming to gender stereotypes?'

Many children in this age group will look at other children

and adults in a binary way; for many there are only boys and girls and men and women, that's it. At this age, many children already have quite stereotypical ideas about how a boy/man and girl/woman should look and behave. If someone deviates from that norm, this person can be 'strange', 'abnormal', or 'weird' in their eyes. Some children at this age have very rigid ideas about what girls and boys should be like and what is expected of them as a boy or a girl. These ideas also have an impact on girls' and boys' self-esteem. Girls at this age often think that they are less capable in sports, mathematics, decision-making and physical strength. They might think this because of the gender messages in our society or the desire at this age to fit in socially and be appreciated by others. In general, their self-esteem is already lower than that of boys.[1]

What is very apparent in numerous research findings[2] is that some boys struggle to deal with their emotions because in certain cultures boys never learn to think about and acknowledge their emotions. They learn from a young age that to do so is not 'masculine'. Whenever a boy of this age in this kind of environment feels an emotion, especially a negative one, they tend to push the emotion away or deal with it in an aggressive manner because aggression is a masculine, highly acceptable form of behaviour among boys and men. Aggression hides weakness and in this kind of environment weakness is perceived negatively for boys and men. However, weakness is a stereotypically acceptable characteristic in girls and women. Implicitly, boys learn that not only weakness but emotions or characteristics that they perceive as 'feminine' are negative for them and negative in general.

Becoming aware of the influence we have on the development of these stereotypical prejudices in our children could be a first step towards breaking down these limiting beliefs. Teaching girls and boys that they have emotions and how to deal with them, teaching them about empathy and its importance for better relationships, and challenging gendered expectations and binary beliefs with boys and girls can help them immensely in growing up kinder, happier and broader in their outlook. Furthermore, by enabling children to think in a less binary way helps them open their minds to people who might not feel comfortable in a binary world and do not want to follow these stereotypical beliefs about gender and norms. Acceptance and respect for everyone who might not fit in the traditional binary boxes makes the world a kinder place for our children to grow up in. Instead of disapproving of or discouraging their stereotyping behaviour, it is much more effective to emphasize children's positive characteristics, which they may feel they have to hide because they are not stereotypically associated with their gender. For example, you could suggest that your son does something caring for his grandparents or a younger sibling or if you have a daughter, you could encourage her to do some sport with her father or big sister in the park. By doing this, your children won't feel judged but encouraged to behave in other ways.

Question 2: 'How much should I explain and what language should I use when describing the genitals?'

At this stage, it is useful for children to know that genitals have formal names and are made up of different parts with various names and functions. Here are some explanations that you can use as a basis for conversations with your child:

The formal name for a boy's genitals is the penis and the top of the penis is called the glans. The glans of a boy's penis and the top of the clitoris in the vulva of a girl are very similar. The glans is very sensitive and when it is touched carefully it can feel good. Under the glans is the shaft and the skin of the shaft is flexible and can be carefully rubbed. Underneath the shaft is what we call the scrotum. This is like a bag with two balls in it, where sperm will be kept once the boy matures. The sperm comes out of the penis through the little opening on top of the glans where the pee also comes out. Sperm can only come out when the penis is erect and hard. We call this an erection. Erections happen many times throughout the day and night but sperm does not always come out. When sperm does come out, we call that ejaculation.

The outer female genitals are called the vulva which consists of two outer lips that cover and protect the rest of the vulva. Inside the outer lips are two inner lips. These two pairs of lips are there to protect the inside of the vulva where there are two openings: the little opening where pee comes out and another opening which is called the vagina. The vagina is the birth channel. Most babies will use this channel to come out of the belly to the outside world when they are born. And finally, at the top of the vulva there is a little bump, which is part of what we call the clitoris. The rest of the clitoris is inside the body behind the lips and the rest of the vulva. This little bump and the rest of the vulva is very sensitive when touched, like the glans on the penis, and it usually creates a very nice feeling when touched.

Question 3: 'Is now the time to talk about puberty?'

Although most girls and boys don't commence puberty before they are ten, a substantial number of children do. To prevent any unpleasant shocks, it is important that children are prepared for the changes that will happen to their bodies. We know from our professional experience that some girls all over the world continue to start their periods with no understanding of menstruation. Can you imagine the fear that this would evoke? And similarly, for boys can you imagine the shame a young boy might feel on discovering his first wet dream if he thinks he has wet the bed like a baby? Telling children ahead of time about the physical changes that are likely to occur over the coming years enables them to avoid being concerned about pubertal development.

The following is an example of a simple explanation about how girls develop that you may wish to adapt for your own use:

Girls' bodies often start to change earlier than boys'. In girls, their nipples will grow a little and they become darker. Later their breasts will grow as well. Girls will get some hair under their armpits and around their vulva. Their body will grow taller and when they are between ten and thirteen years old, most of them will begin to menstruate, although some start earlier or later. This is also called starting their periods. Do you know what that means? It means that one of the egg cells is leaving their body, together with a little tissue and blood. It's perfectly normal and most girls and women will experience this every month, until all the eggs are gone, at around 50 years old.

It is also worth noting that before menstruation starts, girls have some vaginal discharge, which can be confusing or worrying for some. Vaginal discharge is perfectly normal and it is a healthy way of cleaning the vagina. Some parents and carers find that talking about vaginal discharge is a natural way to start to have conversations about puberty.

Here's an example of a simple explanation about how boys develop:

Boys' bodies usually start to change a bit later than girls'. They will first notice that their penis becomes bigger. Also, their hands and feet will grow while the rest of their body might still be small. They get some hair under their armpits as well as on their legs and arms. And then later, when they are around 13 or 14, their body will grow taller and their voice will 'break' to become lower. When boys are between 11 and 16 years old, their body will start to make sperm. The sperm will sometimes leave the penis spontaneously during sleep. This is called a wet dream. This is perfectly normal and many boys and grown-up men experience this during sleep.

Remember to explain that although the ages we have mentioned above apply to most children, they will not apply to everyone because we are all different, so some children start to develop earlier and others later. This is perfectly normal. And importantly, don't forget to give these explanations to both girls and boys as they need to know what can be expected for both sexes.

Question 4: 'How can we talk about privacy with a child of this age?'

If your child is feeling shy about their naked body, it is a good time to talk about privacy. Everybody, including children, has a right to privacy. But how do we explain what privacy is to a child? Here's a suggestion:

> Privacy means that something is especially for you, and only you. You can choose what you want to share and what you want to keep private. For example, sitting on the toilet and peeing and pooping can be private, your genitals can be private and writing in your diary can be private too. Some people call the genitals private parts, meaning these parts of the body are especially for you and no one else. But actually, all parts of your body are private and belong only to you. You decide if you want others to touch or see parts of your body. No one is allowed to touch your body without first checking that you want them to. Sometimes we choose to be private about our bodies when we are away from our house, but at home we might feel that it's okay to be naked. We can choose what we want to keep private and this might change depending on where we are and who we are with.

Question 5: 'How can I promote self-esteem in my child and help them feel proud of their body?'

Whether your child has become shy about their body or not, the most important message at this age should be that their body is wonderful and beautiful. For children, being proud of their own body is an important part of their self-esteem. And, as we have explained before, self-confidence and self-esteem help children to develop their sexuality. Children with low self-esteem are more vulnerable to bullying, sexual harassment and sexual abuse. Parents and carers can still significantly influence their children's self-esteem at this age, positively or negatively, but peers become increasingly important in this regard.[3] Giving compliments, reacting happily and positively and commenting on even the smallest of issues are still important. Your child needs confirmation from you to build their confidence and self-esteem and this can help minimize any negative impacts from peers.

It is also worth noting that children at this stage may begin to strive for some kind of body ideal. From research, we know that girls are more sensitive to negative comments about their physical appearance than boys, but don't underestimate the sensitivity of boys; they too can be worried about their size, their body shape and whether they have the right 'look'. In the coming years, this concern about body image will increase tremendously; a healthy level of positive self-esteem, confidence and body image, can protect children and young people against negative attacks from others.

Equally, children with a physical challenge, chronic illness or disability can be armed with self-esteem and a positive body image. Being satisfied with how you look, being proud of who you are and what you can do are the most important aspects of positive self-esteem and body image. Being positive about your children, giving compliments and teaching them to discover and appreciate the positive sides of themselves are important ingredients of a positive parenting approach. At the end of this chapter you will find an exercise related to building self-esteem that you can do with your child.

Question 6: 'How should I deal with gender exploration in my child?'

An important part of having a positive self-esteem and body image is to be happy and satisfied with your own gender. Some children are not. At around the age of five, when gender identity development becomes increasingly stable, some children discover that although the outside world is calling them 'boy' or 'girl' and although they have the genitals of a boy or girl, they feel confused. Inside they feel more like a different gender and some want to express themselves in this way. They might want to wear clothes and have a hairstyle that is usually worn by the other sex and by the time they reach the age of seven to nine, many have an enduring feeling that they are not the sex assigned to them by birth. This awareness can be very confusing for them. The confusion arises not from the child but from the reaction of the environment that surrounds them. Sometimes their parents might keep emphasizing that they are defined by their biological sex and ignore and completely deny their child's feelings and emotions. If your child insists that they are or want to be another sex at this age, they need support, acceptance and respect for the way they feel about their gender. However, this is not always easy for all parents and carers and we recommend that you seek professional support for both your child and yourself.

Question 7: 'What can I tell my child about how babies are made, pregnancy and birth?'

Children at this age are generally able to understand every detail of the reproductive process, as long as the words used are not too complex. The details of conceiving a baby by intercourse,

IVF, donor conception or surrogacy can be readily outlined by parents, carers and teachers. Adoption can also be explained as can the fact that two fathers, two mothers and single parents can have babies and children. Children at this age can benefit from having their perspectives broadened by learning about families that are different from their own. Here is an example of a conversation between a child and parent about reproduction, pregnancy and birth that you may find useful:

Parent to eight-year-old son: 'Have you seen Auntie Jane's belly recently?'

Child: 'Yes, she is pretty huge. Is she pregnant or has she just had too much cake?'

Parent: 'She's pregnant; her baby will be born next month. You're going to have a cousin. Isn't that exciting?'

Child: 'Yeah, sure. But babies can't play so I'm not sure if this is all that exciting really.'

Parent: 'Has anyone told you how the baby got into Auntie Jane's belly?'

Child: 'Uhhhh…no…I heard some stories from school, that a woman and man have to make love or something?'

Parent: 'Okay, let me tell you the story. Do you want to hear it?'

Child: 'Yes, tell me.'

Parent: 'You already know that men have sperm which is made in their balls or testes, which is the proper name for them. Do you remember?'

Child: 'Yep.'

Parent: 'When you get older, you will start to produce sperm too. Women don't have sperm, but they have egg cells which are kept in their ovaries, which are in their belly. When a man and a woman love each other and want to make love, the man's penis gets bigger and hard and it goes inside the woman's vagina, which is an opening in her vulva.'

Child: 'Yuk, do they really do that? Do they like it?'

Parent: 'Yes, most adults do. We call this having intercourse, having sex or making love. After the penis enters the vagina, it releases sperm, which swims high up into the vagina and enters the woman's uterus. If one of the egg cells is moving around in there, the sperm meets the egg cell. If the sperm enters the egg cell a baby may develop. It will grow in the woman's uterus until it is big enough to be born. And do you know how the baby comes out of the belly?'

Child: 'Yes, I heard it comes out of the vagina.'

Parent: 'Yes, after nine months, most babies come out of the vagina. But some babies don't. When it's not possible for the baby to come out of the vagina, the doctor makes an opening in the woman's belly and takes the baby out.'

Child: 'Cool!'

Parent: 'You were made exactly like this. Your mother and I loved each other so much that we wanted to have you. My sperm and your mother's egg cell came together when we had sex and that's how you started to grow.'

Child: 'Yuk, you really did that together?'

Parent: 'Now you think it is "yuk", but when you are grown up, you might feel differently.'

Child: 'Oh, no, never!!'

Parent: 'Now, here's a question for you. Your Auntie Jane has no husband or boyfriend. She has a girlfriend as her partner. How do you think the baby arrived in her belly?'

Child: 'I dunno…maybe she bought some sperm?'

Parent: 'You're nearly right but not quite. Auntie Jane and her girlfriend met a wonderful man, who was happy to give his sperm to Auntie Jane.'

Child: 'Huhh? How did he do that?'

Parent: 'He put some sperm from his penis into a small jar and gave it to Auntie Jane. Auntie Jane put the sperm into a syringe, like the one you used when you played doctors when you were little. Using the syringe, she put the sperm into her vagina and she became pregnant. That was her greatest wish, to have a baby.'

Child: 'Oh.'

Parent: 'So now you know how a baby is made and how they come out.'

Child: 'Do people who make love together always get pregnant?'

Parent: 'Ah, what a smart question! No, that's not always the case. When two people who want to make love do not want to have a baby, they can use a pill or a condom to prevent the sperm entering the egg cell. If the woman takes a pill every day, there will be no egg cell in her uterus, so the sperm that swims up her vagina into the uterus will not find an egg cell there. The two people could also use a condom. Do you know what a condom is?'

Child: 'Yes, Charlie showed me one in the playground. It looks like a little balloon. Haha!'

Parent: 'Yes, you're right. A condom looks like a little balloon. When the penis grows hard, the condom fits around it and the sperm flows into the condom instead of the woman's vagina. Is there anything else you want to ask? I'll give you a book tomorrow with lots of funny pictures about sperm and egg cells and how they swim together and become a baby. We can read it together if you like.'

Question 8: 'Should children learn about different types of families now?'

There are many advantages to introducing diversity early. By now, most children will have noticed that their friends may live in families that are different to their own; some might live with just their mum or just their dad, two fathers, two mothers or they may live part of the week in one household and the other part of the week in another. Teachers, carers and parents can explain that in many cultures people are free to live in the way that suits them best and that children who grow up outside the traditional family, perhaps with one or two fathers or one or two mothers, can be as happy as children from traditional families.[4] It's also important to explain that not all couples have children, that some couples choose to marry and others just want to live together without being married. Couples can be a man and a woman, or two women or two men. By having these discussions, children are likely to develop respect for others' ideas, values and behaviours even when they are different from their own.

Question 9: 'My child only has one friend. Is that a problem?'

At this stage, children's social networks are expanding rapidly. By interacting with different peers and adults, they may learn more about the principles of effective interaction. Friendships develop in different ways and on different levels now; children at this age can have best friends at the top of the hierarchy, followed by second best, and at the lowest level there will be acquaintances or classmates. Some children have one friend, whereas others have a group of vague friends with more distance, and some children have no friends because they don't yet know how to connect or may be happy to be on their own.

Learning social skills is an essential part of development. Adults can play a huge role in helping children in this regard. You might want to go back to Chapter 4 to see this discussion in detail.

Question 10: 'Can eight year olds be in love?'

Children of this age group may feel something very special for another person. These special feelings can be exciting, confusing and sometimes overwhelming for a child of this age. At this stage, children also become aware of names for this special feeling, such as 'being in love' or 'having a crush'.[5] These feelings are very specific and absolutely real. Children experiment with these feelings and they learn how to deal with them from observing the behaviours of others and from the reaction of the person they love.

At this stage of development, the feelings are not yet fully accompanied by sexual feelings. For most children in this age group, 'being in love' is simply associated with enjoying the presence of the other child and wanting to play with them. For most children, these feelings are positive but our professional experience suggests that some also have negative emotions like nervousness and stress, may find it difficult to sleep and may feel insecure. And when the feeling is not reciprocated, the child can feel deeply hurt and sad.

Question 11: 'I think my son might be in love with a boy. What should I do?'

Research[6] shows that some children will experience the same feelings of love or attraction, described above, for someone of the same sex. Living in a world where the majority of people fall in love with another sex means that these feelings can be very confusing for children at this age. Some do not dare to reveal their feelings to anyone and will hide or deny them for a long time.

If you notice that your child might be confused, depressed or scared by his feelings, try to talk with him. Even if your child is completely denying what he feels, it is important for him to know that you do not condemn or judge his feelings. The best thing to do is to talk in general terms, for example: 'For me, it wouldn't matter who you love or have a crush on. It could be a boy or a girl, it doesn't matter.' Even if your child objects to what you say, perhaps even loudly, if you reassure him he will know that he will be supported by you whenever he is ready to acknowledge his own feelings.

Importantly, remember that trying to change his feelings or change his mind is of no use. This will only become a frustrating fight between you both that will add to his confusion, resulting in unhappiness, self-denial and even more sadness because he will know that you will not accept him as he truly is.

Question 12: 'What messages should I convey about sex at this age?'

Before you start to have these conversations, think through what values you wish to convey. If you think that sex and love are inextricably linked and you say something like: 'You should only have sex with someone you love', you may implicitly suggest that 'sex without love is bad'. If you fully support this value, it's your choice to share this with your child. But if you don't fully agree with this, you may consider changing your message to something like: 'Sex can become more pleasurable when people love each other.'

Regardless of what messages you want to share with your child about sex and sexual relationships, at this age it would be good to emphasize that sex is something for later, for grown-ups, or for when people are old enough for sexual relationships. Children know that this isn't children's stuff, so relating the conversation about sexual behaviour and sexual relationships to something adults can do is much more realistic than just saying: 'This is something you will do when you grow up.' In your message it should be clear that having sex can be a choice and sex and relationships do not necessarily make all people happy.

Question 13: 'Sex is all over the media. How should I deal with it?'

It's true that sex is everywhere, but movies, TV series, music channels or any other media can offer the perfect opportunity to start a conversation about sexuality with your child and counteract some of the messages they will be receiving. Every programme is a great opportunity for a brief conversation or comment. Try to watch your child's favourite shows or music with them when you can and make some comments, both positive and negative, like: 'That's really kind of him' or 'I don't think that's kind. What would you do?' Take the opportunity to challenge damaging messages because at this stage parents are still important role models, so your comments have value and the messages you convey now will be very helpful as your child matures.

Question 14: 'If my children come across porn at this age, what should I do?'

At this age, watching porn, deliberately or accidentally, is not supportive for a child's development and should, therefore, be prevented. Children's internet usage should still be monitored at this age and it is advisable to put limits on the use of devices and the time and place they can be used and to use parent control software to block devices from porn sites.

However, as seen in Chapter 1, with widespread availability of the internet and children's access to digital devices, coming across porn is a very real possibility. If it does happen, don't become angry, but quietly comfort and reassure your child if they have found the images distressing, and explain the principles listed below:

○ It is not for children.

○ These people are all actors; this is not reality.

○ In real life, people show more love, tenderness and kindness to each other when they make love.

○ In most of these films, women are not treated kindly.

○ People's bodies don't usually look like the actors' bodies.

○ Making love or having sex is something which should never be violent or forced.

○ In real life, there is more talking, consent and respect, and everything should stop if a person doesn't want to do something.

Question 15: 'Should I mention that sex can be pleasurable?'

Yes, we think it is important to explain to your child that sex can be pleasurable. But the response to this question warrants a more detailed response than a simple yes or no because sex is only pleasurable when it is completely voluntary, without force or coercion and where it is consensual throughout. In addition, sex will only be pleasurable if it is safe and if there is no fear of unwanted consequences, such as an unplanned pregnancy or a disease. Even then, sex is not always automatically pleasurable and does not necessarily lead to happy and fulfilling relationships.

Question 16: 'How should I talk about boundaries and consent?'

An important aspect of a happy relationship is the respect that partners have for each other's wishes and limits. It takes time for children to understand their own wishes and limits and they learn this through play, for example they might learn whether rough play, like wrestling, is acceptable to them. In the previous chapter, we explained the need for children to think about what they want and don't want in daily life and to learn how to express these feelings. This can be facilitated by giving children simple choices, letting them make simple decisions and allowing them to experience the consequences of their choices. At this stage, this learning remains important and decisions that have long-term consequences are still too difficult for them, but to be able to reflect on what they want and don't want, and to be able to express this, is a first and important step.

A key area of learning to build on at this stage is that children need to know that their body should never be touched against their will. And that they cannot touch another person's body against their will. The #MeToo movement has taught us the importance of being attentive to the wishes and limits of the other person. Although this may not seem relevant to children of this age, this principle applies to all of their friendships and relationships now, and will also be applicable as they mature and develop more intimate relationships. But how can we help children develop these skills? In most cases, all they need to learn to do is ask a question: 'Is it okay if I hold your hand?', 'Do you like this game?' and so on. A simple question is often enough and we can teach them this through the examples we set, by asking children simple questions like: 'Would you like me to hold your hand?', or in a family situation, 'Can I have a kiss?' However, your child also needs to know that asking for permission is not always possible and that being attentive and sensitive to what another person wants and does not want can be necessary too. We address this in Chapter 9.

Question 17: 'How can children learn about good and bad secrets?'

This is a very important area of learning for children at this age as their need for privacy and autonomy develops. Here's an example explanation that you could use as a basis for what you might say:

A good secret is exciting and positive, like a birthday present you have bought for a friend. A bad secret feels awkward and makes you uncomfortable. You should always share these bad secrets with someone else – someone you trust like your parents, carers or a teacher. Examples of bad secrets might be when you have broken a valuable thing which belongs to someone else and you haven't told them yet. Another example is when someone has asked you to touch their body when you don't want to. Or perhaps someone has asked you to do other things that you don't like or don't want to do, like getting you to go inside their house, sitting too close to them or touching you, and this person tells you to keep these things secret. That kind of secret is wrong because it makes you unhappy and uncomfortable. Those situations are never your fault, never. If something like that happens it is always the other person's fault, even if you haven't clearly said no, and it's important that you tell an adult you trust.

Question 18: 'Should I be worried that my children want to play doctor-type games with each other?'

These kinds of games are quite common between siblings at this age but within the family it is very difficult to establish whether consent is complete and participation is entirely voluntary, and siblings at this age won't know either. Having fun together with these games is not always harmful, especially when a parent can keep a watchful eye on them. But unfortunately, we do not know what impact these games can have on the individual child. As adults, some are happy that they had these experiences, but others aren't. In sexual counselling, we sometimes see adults who became sexually aroused by their brother or sister when playing such games and these experiences can have consequences for later sexual relationships. We therefore advise parents and carers to ask siblings to play different kinds of games together.

Question 19: 'How can we protect children against online sexual predators?'

In addition to the measures set out for parents in Question 14, children need to be taught how to use privacy settings on individual apps. Parents, carers and teachers also need to make some agreements with children about how to stay safe on the internet by explaining these rules:

○ Do not accept unknown people on to your games and apps – not everyone on the internet is honest.

○ Remember that some people pretend to be children but really they are adults.

○ Never give your full name, address or mobile number to a friend on the internet.

○ Never share photos with someone you don't know.

○ Only share your first name or a nickname.

○ You can share questions or stories about yourself but be careful not to share people's names or your address or telephone number when telling these stories.

○ If you feel uncomfortable or you don't trust someone, let an adult that you trust know.

○ If you've accidentally done any of these things, let an adult that you trust know.

Children at this age will need regular reinforcement of these messages, and monitoring at home is important.

Question 20: 'What should we tell children about sexual abuse?'

Although this is a difficult topic to discuss, it is extremely important for children to know that some people have bad intentions. Parents, carers and teachers can help children to learn that sometimes a person may seem kind, but they might do things which make them feel uncomfortable. Children should be taught that as soon as they have this feeling, they should listen to their instincts and tell the person that they want to leave and they must tell a trusted adult about what has happened.

To reduce the risk of children encountering this kind of situation, agreeing on rules such as these can be helpful:

○ Always let a trusted adult know where you are.

○ Never go to places which you do not know.

○ If someone asks you to go to their house, even if you have been there before and nothing happened, let your parent or carer know where you are.

○ If something feels uncomfortable, leave the person or the situation. Or tell the person that you have to ask your parent or carer first.

○ If your parent or carer wants you to be picked up from school by another person, they will always let you know. If someone says that your parent or carer has asked them to collect you, check with the teacher.

○ If you are with friends and they want to play or do something which makes you uncomfortable, leave the place.

○ If you are bothered about something that has happened, let your parent or carer know.

○ Remember, if something bad happens in spite of all these agreements, it will not be your fault.

EXERCISE 1: IMPROVING YOUR CHILD'S SELF-ESTEEM

Ask your child to make a list of at least three things they are proud of or like about their physical appearance, for example, 'I am proud of my hair' or 'I am proud of my smile.' And make another list of at least three aspects of their personality they are proud of, such as, 'I am a good listener' or 'I always help my mum when she asks me to do something.' Ask them to make a third list outlining what they are good at and what achievements they are most proud of.

You could also write a list about your child and give this to them as a gift to boost their self-esteem. Your child could also do this exercise with a friend by first making their own lists and then making a list for each other.

EXERCISE 2: EXPRESSING EMOTIONS

Write a poem with your child about any topic related to relationships or sexuality. An easy way to do this is to use the structure of an 'elevenie', which is a short poem with a given pattern. It contains 11 words which are arranged in a specified order over five rows, and on each row a specific number of words can be used:

Row 1: one word (expressing a feeling or emotion)
Row 2: two words
Row 3: three words
Row 4: four words
Row 5: one word (the same word as in the first row).

Here's a beautiful example by a nine-year-old boy about 'Love':

Love
The glow
In your eyes
It's like a sea
Love

Chapter 8

Supporting Children's Development and Learning in Relationships and Sexuality

Ten to Eleven Years

Introduction

By the time children are aged ten to eleven most are about to start, or have started, puberty. Sometimes, in our work with parents, carers and professionals, we notice some confusion between the terms 'puberty' and 'adolescence' and sometimes the terms are used interchangeably. However, there is a difference. Puberty refers to a stage of rapid physical and mental changes which enable physical maturation and, for many people, sexual reproduction. Adolescence is a life stage between childhood and adulthood. Although adolescence usually coincides with the start of puberty, the end of puberty does not mean that adolescence ends too. The World Health Organization defines adolescence as the stage between ten and nineteen years of age, whereas puberty can occur at different times within this timespan.

This chapter is set out in the same way as the previous three chapters and makes use of the international standards listed in Chapter 5. From these guidelines and standards, we have selected themes and topics that we consider important for children to learn about at ten to eleven years. We have matched the topics up with questions from parents, carers, teachers and other professionals and we have provided you with answers. Sometimes we suggest certain words so that you can implement the international guidance, but remember, these are just suggestions and you are free to use whatever words work best for you and your context.

Relationships and sexuality education for ten- and eleven-year-olds

Topics	Questions and answers
The human body and human development	
Puberty changes and body hygiene	Questions 1, 2 and 3
Girls' body changes	Questions 1 and 2
The hymen	Question 3
Boys' body changes	Questions 1 and 4
Sexual gender gap	Question 5
Mental and emotional changes in puberty	Questions 6 and 7
Self-esteem	Question 7
Sexual awareness	Questions 8 and 13

Fertility and reproduction	
Reproduction and family planning	Questions 9 and 10
Contraception	Question 10
Unpleasant consequences of sex	Question 11
Sexuality	
Love feelings	Question 13
Sexual feelings and attraction	Questions 13 and 14
Emotions	
Able to differentiate between emotions	Question 15
Empathy	Question 17
Privacy and respect of others' privacy	Question 16
Relationships and lifestyles	
Importance of friendship	Question 19 and Exercise 2
Healthy and unhealthy friendships	Question 17 and Exercise 3
Fights and quarrels	Question 17
Gender	
Gender roles	Question 12
Social and cultural determinants of sexuality	
Decision-making skills and development of values and norms	Question 18 and Exercise 1
Development of critical thinking	Question 18

Question 1: 'When exactly can I expect puberty to start for my child and how will I know it has begun?'

Although the start of puberty is not a sudden transition in a child's life, usually there are several physical changes which announce its onset (explained in Question 2). Girls generally begin puberty around 18 months to two years earlier than boys. In western European countries, the first signs in girls are observed at around ten years of age. Puberty starts when a complex and subtle balance of weight and height has been reached. This will signal to the pituitary gland, at the base of the brain, that the body is ready to produce a large amount of sex hormones: oestrogen, progesterone and testosterone. The body has been producing these hormones since birth but only at very low levels. The sudden tsunami of sex hormones is the start of several physical and mental changes for children.

Question 2: 'What changes occur in a girl's body at this age?'

Girls start to notice a change in their nipples at around ten years of age and, for some, these changes will start sooner. The nipples become larger and may change in colour. Girls might feel a thickened disc behind the nipples, which may feel sensitive or even painful. This is the start of breast development. After this, pubic hair and hair under the armpits and on the legs will become darker and longer. The pubic hair and armpit hair usually begin as a small number of straight or long hairs which become short, curly and sometimes darker coloured. The bones become heavier and more adipose tissue (body fat) develops on the hips, upper legs and buttocks. The uterus and vagina become larger too, as do the inner and outer vulva lips. The vulva lips also change in colour and they grow in an irregular way, which may lead to longer or uneven inner lips compared with the outer lips. Many girls, if not prepared, will think that they have ugly or abnormal vulva lips and in some western cultures it is not uncommon for young girls to want labia reduction surgery because they think they are the only ones with vulva lips that are long or uneven[1]. In reality, every woman has irregular vulva lips; only pre-pubescent girls have perfectly shaped vulva lips which will neatly close around the vaginal opening.

Girls also start to grow taller now and, within around two to three years of the first signs of puberty, menstruation begins. In western countries, girls begin to menstruate, or start their periods, at around 12 years of age and, contrary to what many people believe, this average age has not declined since 1980.[2] The mean age of the menarche (first menstruation) differs for cultural groups and African American girls tend to commence menstruation about one year earlier than their white peers.[2] It is extremely important that girls are prepared and informed about what happens when they start to menstruate. We see from research that girls who are informed experience less embarrassment and consider menstruation as less dirty or uncomfortable than girls who are not informed.[3]

Often, before menstruation begins (varying from months to years), girls will notice some vaginal discharge. Normal discharge is clear or whitish and won't have much of a smell, and it can leave a yellowish tint on the underwear. Some girls get confused and uncomfortable when they notice their discharge and search on the internet for ways to get rid of it. They should know that it is completely normal and that cleaning the outside of their vulva and in between their vulva lips daily with lukewarm water, without soap, will be enough. Using sprays or cleansers for the inside of their vagina will make the discharge worse and be likely to cause irritation.

Here's an example of a parent talking about menstruation to their ten-year-old daughter, which could also be adapted for telling boys about menstruation:

> In a woman's belly, there is a small organ called the uterus, which is where a baby grows. On both sides of the uterus there are two small tubes, called fallopian tubes, and at the end of these are ovaries. In the ovaries, lots of tiny egg cells wait until it is their turn to be released. An egg cell is released every month and it slowly moves down through the tube into the uterus. During this trip, if the egg cell meets a sperm, they may merge and make the beginnings of a baby. Do you remember me telling you about how a sperm can come into the vagina? But when there is no sperm, the egg cell dies and moves down the vagina. It takes some tissue from the inside of the uterus with it and some blood, which collects in the girl's or woman's knickers. This happens to nearly all girls and this will happen to you sometime over the coming years. It's called menstruation or starting your periods.

At this point, it is likely that your children will have lots of things they want to ask and you may need to repeat elements of this conversation. One of our daughters wanted to know all about how girls catch the blood and was so fascinated by sanitary towels that she wanted to try one out straight-away! If it feels right, you may also want to add something like this:

When a girl starts puberty, her body slowly becomes more like an adult's, which means that her body is getting itself ready to make a baby. But this all happens very slowly and when you start puberty you can carry on behaving like a little girl for as long as you want. You can still play with your toys and sit on my lap and hug and kiss me as often as you like. But, when your first period starts, it's such an important moment that we will celebrate it. We can have lemonade and you can decide what you want me to make for dinner. Okay?

Question 3: 'What should I say about the hymen?'

Many myths exist about the hymen. The most common is that it is a membrane covering the woman's vaginal opening that ruptures on penetration of any object, such as a penis, finger, tampon or sex toy. This is incorrect; there is no such membrane. Instead, there are some loose folds of tissue which form a crescent-shaped ridge along the entrance of the vaginal opening which means that it leaves the rest of the vaginal entrance open. Sometimes the tissue is loose and sometimes it can be a bit tight.

Once you understand what the hymen is, the commonly held notion that it is a tight membrane closing the vaginal opening which needs to be broken by a penis or a finger when penetrated for the first time makes no sense. Don't tell your child these myths because the message will be that their first sexual intercourse will be bloody and painful, which is untrue. And neither is it true that the boy needs to push hard to break the hymen. By telling your children the truth, you will avoid creating unnecessary anxiety about tampon use, sexual exploration and, as they mature, first intercourse.

Question 4: 'What changes happen to a boy's body at this age?'

When boys are around 12 years old, their hands, feet, penis and testicles will start to grow first. If your son is 12 and needs new shoes every three months but is still a small boy, you now know what it means – puberty is starting! Next, his pubic hair, armpit hair and the hair on his arms and legs will also grow; first there will be a few hairs and gradually, curlier, darker and thicker hair will grow. He will now start to grow taller and his voice will start to break. Only at the end of this process, which can take around three years, will the final part, his first ejaculation, occur. The ejaculation (like the first menstruation) is the final stage of pubertal changes, and after this the body will change only marginally up until he is around 18 years old.

The average age of first ejaculation is not very clear, because this is not something boys discuss and share easily with their parents. Ejaculation can happen during sleep (wet dream), although in the Netherlands we know that around 80 per cent of boys have their first ejaculation through masturbation and not during a wet dream.[2]

Here's an example of a parent talking with a child about ejaculation (again remember that although this example is aimed at a boy, it's important for girls to know too):

Child: 'What's a wet dream?'

Parent: 'Good question, I'll answer you now. Can you remember what sperm is?'

Child: 'I don't really know.'

Parent: 'Let me tell you more about it. Boys start to develop sperm in their testes or balls when they are 10 to 14 years old. Every day lots of sperm are developed. Sperm is needed to make a baby when the sperm meets the egg cell in a woman's uterus. Can you remember us talking about this before?'

Child: 'Yeah. When will I have sperm? What does it look like?'

Parent: 'As soon as you enter puberty, and that will be soon, your body will change. Your penis will start to grow and you'll gradually grow more hair under your arms and on your arms, legs and pubic area. You'll develop more muscle, your body will become taller, your voice will lower. Finally, somewhere between your 10th and 14th year, your body will be ready to produce sperm. Do you remember some of this?'

Child: 'Yep.'

Parent: 'Millions of sperm are produced every day. Some of it comes out of the body when the boy or man has an orgasm. Orgasms usually happen when a boy or man has nice feelings about sex; first the penis becomes hard – we call this an erection – and then when these sexual feelings become stronger and when the man stimulates his penis either with his hand or by engaging in sexual behaviour with someone else, he can reach an orgasm. An orgasm is a nice feeling of total stress-release and it causes the sperm to be released from the testicles to mix with some seminal fluid, before it is released out of the penis. This is called ejaculation.'

Child: 'What does it look like?'

Parent: 'It looks like colourless sticky glue. Sometimes just a drop comes out but other times it might be several teaspoons. If this happens at night, during a dream, you might wake up thinking you have wet your bed, but you won't have done. This is called a "wet dream". It's perfectly normal and happens to lots of boys and men.'

Child: 'Every night?'

Parent: 'No, not every night. We're all different. Some boys and men might have wet dreams quite often, but others may only have an orgasm if they rub their penis when they have sexy feelings or when they have sex with someone else.'

Child: 'Oh yeah, my teacher told us something like that.'

Children will, inevitably, react differently to this kind of information but some may be concerned that all of a sudden they will become grown up and this can make them feel overwhelmed. So, it's worth emphasizing that changes are gradual and that regardless of their physical changes, if they want to play young games and have a hug, kiss and a cuddle from their family, that is absolutely fine and normal too.

Question 5: 'If we tell boys about ejaculation we have to discuss sexual feelings and orgasms to explain it, but what about girls, when do they learn about sexual feelings and orgasms?'

This is a great question that highlights the sexual gender gap. Boys learn to enjoy their genitals and their sexual feelings but girls often know little about their genitals and sexual feelings, because we only talk about breast development, vaginal discharge and menstruation. We know from research that although Dutch girls start puberty earlier than boys, they start with sexual behaviour much later than boys.[4, 5] Through working in sexual therapy, we know that many young women have never seen their own vulva, have never touched it and don't know what sexual arousal feels like. In contrast, many boys have experienced sexual arousal by the time they are ten years old.[2] They start to masturbate around this age, they know how to get an orgasm and they know what makes them sexually aroused.

Another reason for this gender gap is the social value in our culture that girls need to be protected against unexpected pregnancy and abuse. This means that most sexuality education messages often focus on protecting girls whereas boys receive implicit messages that they can discover and experiment with sex. The consequence of this kind of sexuality education is that we forget to explain to girls (and boys) how they can become aroused and enjoy this aspect of their sexuality. Our message, therefore, is that we need to discuss sexual feelings with girls at this age too.

Question 6: 'How should I deal with my child's puberty-related mood swings?'

Your child is not only changing physically at this age, but the puberty-related hormones also significantly impact on mood and social perspectives too. Mood swings are common due to sudden hormonal production peaks. The best thing parents can do is to relax and be accepting, although this isn't always easy! Fights and quarrels can easily happen but they rarely offer solutions. Give your child some time to cool down and then start a discussion in a non-aggressive way. Using 'I' terms instead of 'you' terms is always helpful (see Chapter 3 for more tips on communications skills). This is the age at which you, as a parent, should learn to negotiate with your child. Using 'you' terms tends to force the child to defend themselves and soon the conversation will give way to a fight. In negotiating conversations, you explain how you feel when your child screams or yells at you or disobeys you and subsequently you can ask: 'How are we going to solve this situation?' The emphasis is on 'we' rather than 'you'. There are many books and websites that can help you further with this sometimes challenging topic.

Question 7: 'My child doesn't want to "grow up". What can I do?'

Sometimes a child might be experiencing puberty physically, but they may feel much younger emotionally and this may make them fearful of becoming a teenager. In our work as sexuality educators, we have met many pre-teenagers who have high expectations of puberty and adolescence. They think they suddenly have to behave like an adult and won't be allowed to be childish any more. Some say they are afraid that they will suddenly have more responsibilities and more homework and they sometimes worry that parents and friends will expect too much of them; some even fear that they will become lonely or bullied. These concerns can have a negative impact on a child's self-esteem. Explain to your child that regardless of how their body is changing, it's fine to continue to have cuddles from you and to carry on with their favourite hobbies and games, watch the same TV programmes and so on. They can still be themselves, sometimes feeling a bit childish, sometimes behaving like a cool teenager. Children can determine their own pace.

Question 8: 'My daughter's only ten and wants to dress like she's 16. What can I do?'

When your ten-year-old daughter suddenly starts to look like a sexy young woman with a padded bra, make-up, short skirts and crop tops, it can be hard to hide your shock. But this is one of those moments when counting to ten to compose yourself before you speak is invaluable because an outburst is likely to be counterproductive. Keep calm, but you can be firm. If you think your daughter is too young for this at her age, you are well positioned to correct her and tell her your rules, but be aware of your communication skills so that she doesn't feel attacked or humiliated. 'I' terms are particularly useful in these situations, as we have illustrated in the following example of a conversation:

Parent to daughter of ten-year-old wearing heavy make-up, crop top and short skirt: 'Where are you going darling?'

Child: 'I'm going to Elaine's. We're going to watch a movie.'

Parent: 'Why are you wearing make-up?'

Child: 'Because she wears lots of make-up. What's wrong with it?'

Parent: 'It looks beautiful, but I don't want you to wear make-up outside the house.'

Child: 'Why not? Elaine does. Everyone does in my class.'

Parent: 'Darling, I don't care if everyone is doing it. It looks beautiful but I feel worried when I see you looking like this because you look much older than you are and I am afraid that people will treat you like that instead of someone who is ten years old.'

Child: 'What would be the problem? I'd love to be treated like a 16-year-old.'

Parent: 'No you wouldn't. Would you like to throw away all your toys, to study for hours every night, to be refused entry into the McDonald's playground and not be allowed to use the slide in the park any more?'

Child: 'Uuhhh…not really.'

Parent: 'Okay, so take your make-up off and be a ten-year-old girl. Let's agree to allow you to wear make-up at home. Is that okay for you?'

Question 9: 'My child was conceived by artificial insemination. Should I explain it at this age?'

Most children at this age will be able to understand how a baby is made, not only by intercourse but also by other methods such as artificial insemination and surrogacy. They will also be able to understand the different ways a child can come into a family, for example through a vaginal delivery, caesarean section or adoption. You can tell your child how they came into the world and if you have pictures of you or their biological mother when pregnant and a picture of their ultrasound scan, this will help to make the conversation more relatable.

If you haven't yet had the chance to talk about this topic with your child, look for ways to begin the conversation as we suggest in Chapter 3 and have a look through the previous three chapters where we have provided examples of how to talk with children about conception. The UK Donor Conception Network advises having this conversation as early as possible so that children normalize their origins; the same applies for adopted children.

Question 10: 'Should I talk about contraception at this stage?'

It is helpful for children of this age to know about contraception, to help them begin to understand reproductive rights and debunk the widespread belief among children that adults only have sex when they want to make a baby. This conversation offers a gentle way of explaining that sexual intercourse can be pleasurable for grown-ups, and for many people this is a way of expressing their love and appreciation for each other. You can explain that in order to prevent a baby being made every time grown-ups have sexual intercourse, many people use contraception. You can briefly outline that there are lots of different forms of contraception but the most commonly used methods are:

- condoms

- contraceptive pills

- intrauterine devices

- contraceptive implants

- sterilization.

You do not need to go into detail at this stage, but just need to raise your child's awareness. You might also find it useful to phrase this discussion in a more detached way, by saying something like 'people can use…' rather than 'you'. But, children do need to know that once they have their first period or start to ejaculate their body is capable of creating a baby. So, in addition to any personal values you may wish to convey, it is important to emphasize that sexual intercourse is not only for pleasure when you are grown up, but also for making a baby. Children need to understand that intercourse has consequences and using contraception can keep sexual intercourse pleasurable and safe. It is also important to emphasize that contraception should always be the responsibility of both partners.

Question 11: 'I understand that it is important to focus on the pleasurable side of sex, but should I mention potential unpleasant consequences too?'

In addition to learning about preventing unintended pregnancies (see above), it is useful for children to know that sexually transmitted infections can be an unpleasant consequence of unprotected sexual intercourse. At this age, they don't need much detail but they do need to get the message that the best protection against infection is to use a condom. At home, if you want to, you could show them a condom.

In relation to preventing an unplanned pregnancy it would be wise to introduce the use of a condom plus any other safe contraception method (usually the pill). In the home situation, if you want to, you could show your child which contraceptives you use yourself – condoms, the pill or maybe an implant. Depending on your child, you could finish your conversation with a remark like: 'Remember, when you are older and you feel ready to have sex with a boyfriend or girlfriend, I really want you to do it safely, to protect yourself and to protect your partner.

I'll let you know where to find the best type of contraceptives for you. Okay?'

Question 12: 'How can I help my son in not wanting to conform to stereotypical gender behaviours?'

What we see at this age is that most children want to be accepted by their peers. They don't want to be seen as an outsider by being different. It can be very challenging for children to follow their personal beliefs and wishes at this age and they need to be very confident to be able to withstand the potentially negative comments and teasing from classmates. They also need significant support from their parents, carers, teachers and other professionals.

We have observed that it is more socially acceptable for girls to follow their true personal beliefs about what they want to do and look like than it is for boys. For example, a boy who likes to participate in ballet classes is likely to have a more difficult time at this age than girls who choose to join martial arts clubs. Masculinity stereotypically means power and strength and femininity means weakness and softness. Any challenge to these stereotypes can give rise to strong negative reactions among some adults and, sometimes, children. Assumptions may be made about a child's strength or gender affinity and this may give rise to bullying. Supporting your child to become strong, confident and unintimidated by what his classmates think or say, is the ideal situation. But let's also be realistic, many schools will not offer the kind of environment where every child can be completely themselves safely. As long as the child feels safe at home, supported by a family who doesn't want to push them into strict gender roles, they can still explore their potential and their desires.

Here is a true story for you to consider:

My son was almost ten years old and for his birthday we decided to get him a real watch. He was very happy and proud that he could get his first watch, so I asked him to accompany me to the shop to choose it himself. In the shop, the female shop assistant showed him several colourful children's watches. They looked lovely and my son was delighted. 'Which colour do you want?' the shop assistant asked him. After some thought, he said: 'I think the pink one is the most beautiful.' Although the shop assistant and I didn't react, we were both thinking the same thought: *Mmmhh…pink is a girl's colour. What will the children in his class say when they see him wearing a pink watch?* I didn't know what to say; I wanted to give him his dream watch but I was scared that he would be laughed at and bullied at school. The shop assistant could see my struggle and said: 'That is a lovely colour you have chosen. I really like your choice. This one is the most popular watch in our store, especially with girls. You are the first boy to like the pink one. All the girls in your class will love your choice.' My son looked at her and understood the message; he chose a green one.

This true example, used in our training sessions, always evokes much discussion. Some adults strongly object to the solution and emphasize that the child should not have to adapt and hide his true wishes. Instead, society should adapt and learn to accept children with different preferences. Others agree with the way the child was gently guided to adapt himself to society. It's a difficult dilemma, especially when it concerns your own child. In Chapter 9, when discussing the Flag System, we will come back to a similar dilemma and use the criteria of the Flag System to argue why protecting a child against ridicule can sometimes be the right decision.

Question 13: 'Does "falling in love" have sexual connotations for children at this age?'

For some children at this age, feelings of love become more associated with sexual feelings. This is related to the high production of sex hormones associated with puberty. In the previous chapter, we explained that research[6] has shown that for most children, feelings of love have nothing to do with sex or sexual behaviours; they just want to be close to each other. But at this age, children report that they get a certain feeling in their stomach and in their genitals when the child they love is very close. The need to touch and have some skin contact becomes greater and more obvious. If you observe children in the playground at this age, you'll see that although the two sexes often play in separate groups they watch each other closely and when they do play together the games involve touch, for example tag, cops and robbers or kiss chase. When the feelings of love are mutual, the two children now not only want to be close to each other but a simple touch when sitting next to each other on the couch can give feelings like 'electric shocks' and this is what they will look for.

Research[4] demonstrates that sexual intercourse at this age, when both children are of the same age, is very rare in western European countries. However, more advanced sexual behaviour beyond holding hands or a quick kiss can occur if one of the two children is several years older than the other. In this situation, attention is required as the older child is at a different developmental level in their sexuality than the younger child, they have different sexual needs and can, by virtue of their age, be more intimidating or persuasive. An age difference can create a power imbalance which can be detrimental to the well-being of the younger child.

Communicating with children about what they want and do not want in the context of sexual behaviour is important in teaching them about boundaries at this stage. Asking the child whether they know what children do when they are in love can help to address any myths or incorrect expectations. Remember that children may have seen porn by this stage and some children may want to boast about how much they have seen or have done. Peer pressure can be very strong now and some children may be made to feel that they are too childish because of their boasting classmates. You can tell your child that boasting doesn't mean that what their peers say is necessarily true and you can also correct any misperceptions about what is usual behaviour at this age and about pornography, as we discussed in the previous chapter.

In relation to individual sexual behaviours, boys might have sexual fantasies and some start to deliberately masturbate at this age. Girls have increased sexual feelings and fantasies too, but are less comfortable with them and more inclined to turn these fantasies into romantic ones, which are considered more acceptable for girls. They like to watch and discuss romantic movies and romantic intrigues with their peers in the school playground and, in this way, they learn to link their sexual feelings to romantic situations. Explaining to girls (and boys) that masturbation is okay, that sexual feelings are okay, and that condemning girls who are clear about their own sexual desires is not okay, can contribute to more equal sexual development of boys and girls.

Question 14: 'Is attraction to the same sex "real" at this age?'

Some children cannot identify with their classmates' stories about their interest in another sex. Some boys do not like 'sexy' pictures of girls and discover they are more attracted to pictures of men. Equally, some girls discover at this age that they aren't interested in their classmates' make-up parties and they don't feel anything for the romantic prince in movies. Instead, they feel special feelings for the princess dancing around the ballroom floor. Children who have these feelings can become very confused because they suddenly feel very different from their friends and classmates. Some will become shy and withdrawn and some hope that this will change as they grow older. Children at this age just want to be like their peers; they don't want to stand out or become the centre of judgemental attention and bullying.

From a research[7, 8] perspective, when we look at young gay adolescents' reports of coming-out, we notice that when they reflect on their childhoods, many of them experienced their first feelings of same-sex attraction between the ages of nine and twelve. Some report having noticed being different from others in their class, but most did not link their feelings to possible homosexuality.

If your child is experiencing these feelings, they will need your positive attention, warmth and love because they are likely to feel lonely and insecure. If your child is aware that homosexuality or bisexuality is taboo or is disapproved of within the family environment, this loneliness and sense of 'abnormality' will be increased. Take care to show your child that you love them unconditionally and if you, other members of the family or your child are struggling emotionally, seek professional support.

One final point to mention here is that at this age some children discover that they become sexually aroused by sexual images of people of the same sex. This can be confusing for them, especially if they do not feel any love or romantic attraction to someone of the same sex. If this applies to your child, you can explain that becoming aroused is sometimes purely a physical process and the mind does not always have immediate control over the physical reaction. In other words, the body is not thinking, it is just reacting spontaneously, and these feelings do not necessarily mean that a child is homosexual.

Question 15: 'How can I help my child express their emotions?'

The tips that we have suggested in the previous chapters still apply at this age, but most children will now be able to differentiate between different kinds of emotions and will be better able to label them. In addition to these strategies, some children find writing a diary a very useful outlet to express and make sense of their emotions, especially confusing and negative ones which are difficult to share with others. A child's diary must be private though and it is important that everyone respects the child's privacy otherwise they will cease to use it to vent their new and sometimes embarrassing feelings. Another suggestion is to provide children with books about puberty and to discuss how they feel as you go through the books together.

Question 16: 'How much privacy does a child need at this age and how can I explain that others need privacy too?'

Having sexual feelings and exploring the body is perfectly normal for boys and girls at this age. Give your child some space and privacy now. Don't interrupt when they are in the shower or bathroom and don't object if they don't want you around when they want to undress. Your child may now want to have their own room or at least some private space and, if you have room in your house, it is helpful if this can be respected. Some children even want to have a lock on their bedroom door and they put a sign up saying to knock before entering. That's exactly what parents and carers should do from now on; knocking before entering means you respect your child's need for privacy.

This also means that parents and carers should respect their child's privacy in relation to their diary, private notebooks and secret notes on the computer or a mobile. These are all private property and belong to the private space of the child. Sometimes parents wonder if they should check their child's social media accounts for safety reasons. This is completely understandable, but not very wise. For a child of ten and older, discovering that an adult has been reading their private messages can feel like an enormous violation and it can cause a breakdown in trust as the child feels that their parents are spying on them. Communicating with your child about the possible consequences of revealing too much personal information on social media is much better at this stage.

With regards to respecting others' privacy, explain to your child that in the same way that you respect their privacy, they need to respect others' privacy too. This means knocking on the door of a sibling's bedroom or the bathroom before entering, but it also means not sharing pictures or personal data of other people, such as siblings, friends, classmates or peers on social media.

Question 17: 'Should I interfere with my child's friendships at this age?'

Children at this age are better able to reflect more specifically and deeply about friendship qualities and most will be able to evaluate concepts such as loyalty, trust, the ability to give, honesty and so on. They are, therefore, likely to be able to decide what kinds of qualities they value in a friendship for themselves now, although they may still need your support (see Exercise 3).

At this stage, children can learn that even in the best relationships, quarrels and disagreements occur and if people are able to deal with arguments, it doesn't have to have a negative influence on the friendship or relationship. If you notice that your child is not yet able to solve such situations with a friend, offer your help and ask them whether you can discuss the situation and help them look for solutions. Don't overwhelm your child with suggestions; this won't help. Instead, encourage them to come up with potential solutions and list the pros and cons of all their ideas, including the possible consequences of each solution. Then encourage them to decide their course of action and let them go ahead and see if it works.

Positive communication, empathy, the ability to deal with negative emotions and a willingness to cooperate in finding a solution together are key to dealing with quarrels and disagreements. In other words, emotional intelligence is required.

In Chapter 4, we talked about emotional intelligence and you may find it useful to have a quick read of that section again.

But what if your child's friend shows behaviours or expresses values which go against yours? At this age, it is worthwhile discussing your concerns with your child, but this can be a sensitive discussion. If you judge the friend too harshly, your child might consider this a judgement on them. Try to find clear, concrete examples of a situation where you didn't like the specific behaviours or words the friend used and keep the discussion centred on this. Even if your child is offended or shrugs off your comments, everything you have said will have been noted. Your views, as a parent, are still extremely important to your child and most children still want their parent's full approval at this stage. By gently showing your disapproval you will have made your child think, and this is exactly what you want.

Question 18: 'How can we help children in developing their decision-making skills?'

Children at this age are increasingly developing their own opinions, values and personal ideas about everything, including sexuality-related topics. This is a very important aspect of development since it underpins decision-making now and, as they grow up, it will also underpin their sexual decision-making.

At this stage, children need to learn that decisions have consequences. Up until recently, children's opinions and values will have broadly mirrored their parents'. But now, some new values will be acquired from the media and friends. To help children in developing their own values and norms related to sexuality, you can play discussion games. Asking simple questions during dinner or while watching TV or movies together, such as: 'Do you agree with what he did there?' or 'Would you do that?' is an excellent way to develop your child's ability to formulate arguments about relationships and sexuality and to explore the consequences of different decisions.

Critical thinking is also key to decision-making. Children can be helped in developing this skill by being given opportunities to think through their ideas and to support them with good arguments. By doing this, children can explore their own values and take decisions based on these. At this stage, children's values and opinions may begin to deviate from those of the adults in their lives. Challenging their ideas by asking questions helps children learn to reflect on their ideas and adapt or confirm them. However, be aware that being too judgemental, showing disapproval or being dismissive is likely to mean that children may be reluctant to share their thoughts with you in the future, whereas a respectful two-way discussion can be a very positive, bonding experience for both the adult and child, even if your views are in opposition.

EXERCISE 1: BOOKS AND MOVIES

Reading books and watching movies together offers great opportunities for discussing values and opinions.

Discussing the storyline and specific characters or situations together can help children explore their personal values and opinions. Avoid being judgemental or disapproving and stay open minded and show curiosity. Children will appreciate being heard and respected.

EXERCISE 2: IMPORTANT PEOPLE AROUND ME

This exercise can help to make your child aware of the importance of social contacts and where to go for help.

Encourage the child to draw a big flower with six petals, like this:

In the centre of the flower the child can write their name. Each petal presents a category, such as friends, family, neighbourhood, school, home and club/hobby. Ask the child to write the names of people who are important to them in each petal. Then, explore why these people are special or important to them and which of these people would be best to turn to for help.

EXERCISE 3: FRIENDSHIP QUALITIES

To help your child reflect on qualities that they value in a relationship, make a list of around ten important qualities (there are some suggestions below) and leave extra room for several more. Encourage your child to select at least seven qualities which they consider to be the most important in a friendship. Then, ask them to reflect on whether their best friend really possesses all these qualities. After this, ask your child if they possess these qualities as well and, if not, what might they change? Encourage your child to think about any specific aspects that they really don't like or feel comfortable with in a friendship. They can write this down too. Taking time to think about these things can be very valuable. If your child is capable of doing this at this age with your support, it will be of great help in future relationships.

Quality	Important or not?
Trustworthiness	
Honesty	
Sharing the same hobbies	
Funny	
Good listener	
Supportive	
Self-confident	

Same sense of humour	
Kind	
Has fun ideas	

Chapter 9

'Is this Okay?'

Have you ever wondered whether it is okay for a four-year-old to be grabbing his mother's breasts or for a nine-year-old to show his penis in public? One of the most challenging aspects of relationships and sexuality education for parents, carers and professionals alike is knowing what is 'okay' or acceptable sexual play and what isn't. People have very different opinions about what is acceptable sexual behaviour, and cultural perspectives often play a big role in this.

In this chapter, we explore how we can determine what's acceptable and unacceptable sexual behaviour, without solely relying on (or denying) our personal convictions. A very useful resource in helping determine what's acceptable and what isn't is the Flag System, developed by Erika Frans and Sensoa.[1] Although the Flag System was primarily developed for professionals, we have found that it is helpful for parents and carers too. This chapter introduces the system and discusses how you can use it. To obtain the full resource, please see the note in the reference section at the end of this book.

The Flag System's aims

The Flag System is designed to enable adults to correctly assess acceptable and unacceptable sexual behaviour in children and young people aged 0–18 years. The system gives objective criteria based on research to develop our judgement in a more objective way and tries to enable users to put aside their gut reactions which may cloud objectivity. The system also suggests appropriate responses with the aim of promoting healthy sexual development.

As we have discussed in the previous chapters, we observe sexual behaviour with children from birth. Children exhibit this behaviour at home, but also at kindergarten, school, in play-grounds, sport clubs and wherever else they spend their time. In most countries, the general belief is that parents are entitled to deal with this behaviour in the way they see fit. However, professionals need to be able to clearly communicate and justify their response to parents and colleagues. For this reason, the Flag System is now widely used by professionals across Europe who work in a variety of settings, such as care, education, social work and sport, to discuss sexually (un)acceptable behaviour with co-workers, management, parents, carers and with the children and young people themselves. Increasingly it is also being used by parents because of its practical nature.

The Flag System is designed to provide answers to important questions such as:

- How do we know what is okay and what is not?

- How should we judge?

- How should we respond?

It aims to contribute to children's healthy sexual development and to prevent sexual coercion. Using the Flag System creates room for positive sexual behaviour; simply banning sexual behaviour is never a solution.

How it works

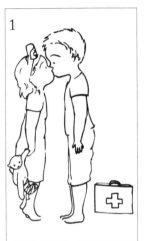

In the pictures above you will see some behaviours that children might exhibit at home, at school or elsewhere. They show:

1. two five year olds playing mummy and daddy in a quiet corner of the house and they are giving each other a kiss on the mouth

2. a three-year-old peeping under an adult's skirt

3. four ten-year-old boys repeatedly bothering other children with sexually suggestive gestures and 'jokes', who, even after being corrected, continue to exhibit this behaviour when they are unsupervised

4. a six-year-old boy who wants to wear a dress to school.

Here's an exercise for you:

- Make a judgement regarding the acceptability or otherwise of the above behaviours.
- Think through how you came to this judgement.

It is likely that your reaction was based on a gut response and, perhaps, some past experience or some understandings regarding what is 'normal' behaviour at different stages of development. The Flag System aims to remove the instinctive element of our natural response and gives us six criteria we can use to assess which behaviours are okay and which aren't. Please note that these descriptions are an overview and if you want to learn more we recommend you read the full Sensoa Flag System.[1]

The first criterion is *mutual consent*, which means mutual agreement. Both parties must give their full and conscious permission. If one party leaves the other in any uncertainty, misleads, cheats or overwhelms the other, consent cannot be assumed. The difficulty with this criterion is that consent is often given non-verbally and people can change their mind once they are engaged in the situation. This is something both parties have to be mindful of. In relation to young children's relationships and sexuality education, adults need to teach children to interpret signals clearly and give clear signals themselves. And of course, we need to teach children to stop if the other party changes their mind. You can introduce this concept from a very young age through play and through teaching children about boundaries (see Chapter 6).

The second criterion is *voluntary engagement*, which is concerned with the individual's willingness to participate. At first, this criterion might seem similar to mutual consent. However, consent is about giving permission to someone else, voluntary engagement is about what the individual really wants. When a child concedes to sexual behaviour that he does not want, there is no voluntary engagement. For example, if a boy agrees to show his penis to some other boys because he is afraid of being laughed at if he refuses, this is not voluntary engagement. Subtle forms of coercion and force, such as persuasion and manipulation, can lead to involuntary engagement. You can't always see whether this criterion is met, so you often have to ask questions. It is important to realize that only the individual involved in the situation can assess whether their personal participation is really voluntary.

The third criterion is *equality*. In sexual behaviour, both parties must be evenly matched, so that one doesn't dominate the other. Both must have equal power within the relationship without being controlled or coerced by the other. So, there must be balance between both parties in terms of age, knowledge, intelligence, power, maturity and status.

The fourth criterion is assessing if the behaviour is *appropriate for the child's stage of development or age*. The focus here is on determining whether the sexual behaviour that the child exhibits might be expected for their age as well as their biological, psychological, social and emotional stage of development. This isn't something you can easily see or check, as it requires knowledge about sexual development. Chapters 5–8 of this book are very helpful in this regard.

The fifth criterion is checking whether the behaviour is *appropriate within the context*. Healthy sexual behaviour in the wrong context can be shocking or insulting, for example the same sexual behaviour might be acceptable in the privacy of one's bedroom but not in school. In practice, we have found this the most challenging criterion because cultural differences can lead to different assessments. For example, when teaching about the Flag System, we have found that participants can argue quite ferociously about the appropriateness of brothers and sisters kissing each other on the lips. For some participants, this would never be appropriate in any circumstance even when all other criteria are met, whereas others see no issue with this.

The sixth and final criterion is *self-respect*. This criterion promotes the importance of children not harming themselves through their behaviours. Sexual behaviour can be harmful physically, psychologically and socially, and children may feel humiliated and get hurt physically and emotionally by getting involved in risky situations.

Here's a second exercise for you to do:

- Return to the situations we outlined at the beginning of the chapter and apply the Flag System criteria to determine how acceptable or otherwise you consider these behaviours to be.

- Have your assessments of the situations changed?

Asking yourself questions as to whether the criteria are met is a good way to analyse what's really going on. It helps you to question your gut feeling and consider whether you are being too relaxed, overly anxious or reacting too harshly. Checking all the criteria also helps a great deal when discussing the situation with a colleague or partner.

But it is unlikely that you will really know all that has happened in a situation, because you may have only witnessed a snapshot or perhaps the situation wasn't clear when you observed it. For example, it is hard to hear whispered exchanges or to know what conversations have occurred through direct messaging. In this case, it is necessary to ask questions to clarify exactly what happened. Although you will probably experience an array of thoughts and feelings when trying to ascertain the facts, it is important to try not to judge at this time. By suspending your assumptions and putting your emotions to one side you're more likely to discover the truth and to respond more appropriately.

The four flags

Once you have accurately determined what has happened

(which probably wasn't easy!) you need to assess to what extent the behaviour is problematic. The aim of this assessment is not to judge the participants, but to determine how you should react. The idea is that by adopting a consistent informed response, children will benefit developmentally. They should feel better able to trust the adults in their lives to make reasoned decisions and to give good advice and they should be better able to set and respect boundaries. So, before telling you a little more about appropriate responses, let's first focus on the four flags.

The green flag

If all of the criteria are met, the behaviour is given a *green flag*. But, if one or more criteria isn't met, the behaviour will warrant a yellow, red or black flag instead. What is important to note here is that it is not the number of criteria that determine if a yellow, red or black flag is given, but it is the degree of unacceptability that is key. In the coming paragraphs this will become clearer.

The yellow flag

Moderately unacceptable behaviour gets a *yellow flag*. An example may be when there is no clear mutual consent or when the behaviour is not completely appropriate within the context. It is important to realize that yellow flag behaviour is quite normal in the development of healthy sexual behaviour, because exploration is a normal part of development, and understanding what an appropriate context is, like all other aspects of social development, must be learned.

The red flag

When we come across seriously unacceptable behaviour, we assign a *red flag*. This is applied when one of the first three criteria (mutual consent, voluntary engagement and equality) clearly isn't met. Another example when a red flag applies is when you observe sexual behaviour that is unusual for the age of the child. This type of behaviour could lead to significant mental (or physical) damage or harm. In addition, yellow behaviour that occurs repeatedly, even when addressed, also gets a red flag.

The black flag

A *black flag* is assigned when you come across very seriously unacceptable behaviour. For example, when the sexual contact is forced with threats, aggression or violence, or when there is great inequality between the two participants.

How to respond

Green flag behaviour should be given space as it is part of healthy sexual development. With this type of behaviour you don't always have to react immediately and you may consciously choose not to react at all. Sometimes, though, it is good to respond because children can learn from your response, so you may choose to name what you saw and perhaps use it to prompt a conversation. Examples might be:

'Did you enjoy cuddling your friend?'

'I heard you had a lot of fun upstairs, what kind of game were you playing?'

'It's good that you only do that in private.'

By doing this, adults can help children learn to talk about sexual behaviour. It also shows children that adults are happy to talk about these kinds of things with them and that they are there for them if they have any questions or concerns. Don't be concerned that you have to give advice to prevent green flag behaviour escalating; most behaviours will stop on their own and if something does escalate, it is better for you to respond separately.

When a yellow, red or black flag is assigned, you should immediately stop the behaviour. With yellow flag behaviour, this can be achieved by distracting a child, but sometimes it is better to name the behaviour and explain which boundary is being crossed and what they can do differently. Some examples are:

'I heard from Michael that you pulled his swimming trunks off; he doesn't like that.'

'You are touching my breasts. I don't like you doing this without asking.'

With red flag behaviour, the priority is to stop it, but the next steps are no different from yellow flag behaviour. You describe what you have seen, you state which boundaries have been crossed and you discuss what the children should do differently. Because red flag behaviour is more serious, you have to make sure that children understand the ban and the consequences. Fortunately, red flag behaviour is not something all children and adults will have to deal with. It is not rare, but it is not a part of most children's development either. We give you two examples of red flag situations and a summary of appropriate responses below. The first example comes directly from the Sensoa Flag System:

Situation: A four-year-old boy tells his mum that a girl has pushed a pencil up his anus while playing doctors. The boy's mother ascertains that this is true.

Potential response from mother to the girl: 'I heard you stuck a pencil up Jack's bottom. You are allowed to play doctors, but you shouldn't hurt anyone. Sticking a pencil into somebody can be dangerous, so you are never allowed to do that.' The mother also attends to Jack: 'I heard Mia stuck a pencil up your bottom. Did it hurt?' The mother waits for a response and comforts Jack, then continues: 'Children should never push objects into each other's body; that can be dangerous. You are in charge of your body and nobody should touch your body without your permission.'

Jack's mother may also decide to discuss what happened with Mia's mother and explain the way she handled the situation.

Here's another example:

Situation: A father hears his ten-year-old son and his three friends of the same age arguing about showing their penises to each other. He hears one boy, Sam, saying that he doesn't want to do this and he hears the others respond by calling him a baby and one boy suggests that they should hold his arms so they can pull his trousers down.

Father's response: The father intervenes immediately and stops the behaviour. First, he comforts Sam, out of sight of the other boys. He explains that it is okay to engage in such activities but forcing someone is absolutely unacceptable. He explains to Sam that he was right to say no and that he has done nothing wrong. The father also contacts Sam's parents as this was likely to have been upsetting for him. Separately he says to the boys: 'You were trying to force Sam to show his penis by making fun of him and even suggested holding him and removing his pants. Why did you do that? How do you think Sam felt when you did that? It is okay to be curious about each other's bodies but forcing someone to take part is absolutely unacceptable. You are never allowed to use physical force or teasing to bully someone into engaging in sexual activities against their will. What you did was very wrong. How can we make sure this doesn't happen again?'

If you are likely to have to deal with red flag situations, we recommend that you discuss the situation with professionals and read the full Flag System book.

Black flag behaviour is not expected to be seen between young children of an approximately equal age and stage of development. It is important to note that black flag behaviour involves illegal action and is not something you should deal with on your own. For this reason, we have chosen not to give examples as this could give the impression that this is straightforward. If you witness a black flag situation, we advise you to seek professional support.

Putting this into action

Let's go back to the exercises at the beginning of this chapter. Consider the three situations again and ask yourself:

- Are all six criteria met?

- If they aren't, to what extent is each criterion not met?

- Which flag do you think best fits the situation?

- How can you respond?

Drawing on the flag system's guidance, let's appraise each situation.

Two five year olds playing mummy and daddy in a quiet corner of the house and they are giving each other a kiss on the mouth

All criteria are met; this is a green flag situation. You don't need to respond, but if you do, it should be positive. For example: 'Was it fun playing mums and dads? Did you enjoy giving him a little kiss? It's fun to play mums and dads and kissing is nice as long as you both like it.'

A three-year-old peeps under an adult's skirt

Almost all criteria are not met: there is no consent, no voluntary engagement on the part of the adult and the context doesn't allow this behaviour. However, the behaviour is quite common and understandable at this age. When we consider to what extent each criterion is not met we ascertain that this is not a serious breach of each criterion. This is a yellow flag situation. This is normal behaviour, but it is important to set boundaries. You could start by taking the child aside and saying something like: 'You are not allowed to look up someone's skirt, and definitely not without asking first.'

Four ten-year-old boys repeatedly bothering other children with sexually suggestive gestures and 'jokes', who, even after being corrected, continue to exhibit this behaviour when they are unsupervised

No criteria are met; there is no consent, no voluntary engagement and no equality because the boys are in a group. While showing off is part of development, it should not create victims. The other children might feel anxious and the boys could get a bad reputation or be sanctioned, so self-respect is also at stake. This is a red flag situation but if it was the first time they had shown this behaviour, it would have been yellow. Your response could be something like this: 'You are making sexual gestures and jokes; other children don't like it. We have already asked you to stop doing this. I am concerned about the fact that you continue to do this when you are not being supervised. It is okay to make other jokes, but it is not okay to bother other children, they don't feel comfortable with you doing this. This must not happen again. Is this agreed? If this happens once more, I will sanction you by…'

A six-year-old boy wants to wear a dress to school

This situation tends to pose a dilemma for parents. What should parents do? When we look at the Flag System criteria, most of the criteria are met: voluntary behaviour, consent and for some children at this age, this is what they want so we could consider it age-appropriate behaviour. But for the next two criteria, equality and self-respect, whether the criteria are met is not so clear. If the other children in school are accepting of his behaviour there will be equality and no risks for his self-respect. But in many schools, this ideal situation does not yet exist. Children who look or behave differently become vulnerable to bullying and this is likely to have an adverse impact on their self-esteem. In this situation, this example would get a yellow flag, because there is potential to start a discussion with the school, including the child's teacher and classmates. But if the school and teacher are supportive and the child's classmates are tolerant of diversity, this situation would get a green flag.

In the yellow flag situation, the parent could say something like this to the child: 'For us, it's okay if you want to wear a dress to school. But what do you think the other children might think and how might they react to you? If you think that the other children will tease you or laugh at you, it's not a good idea. Let me talk to your teacher first to see if she will talk to your classmates about accepting everyone regardless of how they choose to look and act. Is that okay for you?'

You may have been surprised at our application of the criteria in these examples but we hope our explanations will have helped you understand why we have come to these conclusions and recommendations. To help you put the Flag System into action here are a few more examples.

A four-year-old girl plays with her genitals when she is in the bath

In this situation, all criteria are met. This behaviour is appropriate for her age and the context of a private bathroom is suitable. A green flag applies. If you were to walk in and see this behaviour, you could either ignore it or say something positive like: 'I see you are touching your vulva (or whatever name you use at home). Are you enjoying how it feels?'

A few six-year-olds are playing together and you hear them repeatedly saying 'piss', 'poop', 'tits' and so on. They are all really having fun

At least five criteria are met. Having fun is a good indicator of consent and voluntary agreement. The behaviour is normal for their age and there is no problem regarding equality. There is also no risk of physical or psychological harm. The only thing we could question is whether this behaviour is appropriate for the context. Can other people hear them and be disturbed by it or are they standing somewhere private? In view of the last question, we would assess this situation as a green or yellow flag.

You could respond by either ignoring the children or if you think this behaviour is inappropriate for the context, because others can hear it and might find it offensive you could say something like: 'I can hear you saying dirty words. Your language is unacceptable. You can only joke like this when there aren't other people around. If people hear you, they might be offended.'

Our experiences

A common mistake after being introduced to the Flag System, is to use parts of it instead of following all the steps. We see this a lot during training sessions. When we give scenarios to participants, they often assign flags without first using the criteria. As a result, they are guided by their gut instinct rather than objectivity. Frequently we hear: 'I think it's a red flag' but when we say: 'Okay, tell us why, which criteria aren't met?' the response is usually: 'Hmmm, I don't know, none actually.' More often than not, when participants go back and review the scenario against the criteria, the red flag becomes green or yellow.

Even if the steps are followed, it is worth noting that dilemmas can still arise. As we mentioned earlier, we have found that people experience difficulties in interpreting the appropriateness of behaviours within different contexts. This is often due to cultural differences, but within any culture there are variations with communities, families and individuals having their own norms. So, what happens if you feel very strongly that the context makes the behaviour unacceptable? Especially if the context is very nuanced and particular? The Flag System states that a dilemma regarding appropriateness within a certain context can shift the colour of the flag by one, for example from green to yellow, but not from green to red. So there is some room for personal opinions in the Flag System, although this is purposely limited.

Another dilemma that has arisen during training is that people can be inclined to change their response out of concern for what other adults, especially parents, might think of them. A good example is a situation where a couple of three-year-olds are having fun, playing naked 'pile on' in one of their bedrooms.

Most people initially score this situation green, which is correct, but they want to change it out of concern for what other parents might say if they saw this behaviour.

A real strength of the Flag System that parents have reported to us is that the criteria can be applied to other aspects of children's social development. For example, criteria like mutual consent or equality are relevant to other non-sexual behaviours. Applying this approach to everyday life can normalize relationships and sexuality education because the 'rules' are consistent across all aspects of the child's development. For example, when children take each other's toys without asking or when pressure is put on a child by three other children to play hide and seek, the same principles apply. When we realize this, relationships and sexuality education stops being quite so different and separate from other aspects of rearing children.

Summary

Using the Flag System correctly isn't easy because of the nature of the subject, but even a brief introduction like this can help adults rethink relationships and sexuality education. If you are keen to start using the system, particularly in a professional context, we recommend that you take a look at https://flagsystem.org, www.sensoa.be, www.vlaggensyteem.nl or obtain the Sensoa Flag System book.[1]

Chapter 10

What Next?

Your beliefs and behaviours

So, you've got to the end of the book but how has it affected you? Has it changed how you consider relationships and sexuality as a topic for young children? Has it had an impact on how you will approach sexuality and relationships education in your family or professional life?

In Chapter 1, we encouraged you to complete a questionnaire. We would like you to repeat this exercise now. Remember, throughout the questions we have referred to the child or children you'll be thinking of as 'they' but you may be thinking about just one child, perhaps your own child or grandchild or you may be thinking about a whole class full of children or perhaps a caseload – just personalize the questions to you and your context:

1. Do you know the names of three children they have a good relationship with?

   a. Yes, the names are...

   b. I know just one name, but not any others

   c. No, I don't know any names

2. Do you know when they are unhappy at school or pre-school?

   a. Yes

   b. Sometimes

   c. No

3. Do you talk every day about what happened at school or pre-school?

   a. Yes, every day

   b. Sometimes

   c. No, hardly ever

4. Do you know what they are doing on social media? (If they are too young for social media, just skip this question.)

   a. Yes, exactly

   b. Not everything, but enough

   c. No, that is private for them

5. Do you know what they already know about sexuality?

    a. At least everything I have told them

    b. Not much, they are too young for this

    c. I don't know what they know

6. Do you ever talk with them about relationships and sexuality?

    a. Yes

    b. Never

7. If they have questions about relationships and sexuality issues, do they know where to get answers?

    a. Yes, they come to me

    b. I assume they know

    c. I don't know where they get their information from

8. Do you have any books available for them to learn about relationships and sexuality?

    a. Yes

    b. No

9. If you were to discover they have a problem with sexuality or if they demonstrate problematic sexual behaviour, do you know where to go to for help?

    a. Yes, I know

    b. No, I don't know

10. Do you know their opinions about teenage pregnancy, contraception, sexual diversity and masturbation? (If they are too young for these topics, just skip this question.)

    a. Yes, because we talk about these things

    b. I have no idea if they are thinking about these topics

Now return to the answers you gave in Chapter 1. Have your responses changed in any way? If so, how?

In making sense of why some of your responses may have changed, it may be helpful to recap on some of the themes that we have introduced throughout the book. We have proposed that relationships and sexuality communication:

• can be an integral part of everyday life

• requires some thought but doesn't need to be difficult or awkward

• needs to be developmentally appropriate

• is a child's right

• can be protective for children

• can be fun.

We have also argued that it is impossible to shield children from learning about relationships and sexuality even if adults choose not to discuss these issues with them directly. We, therefore, propose that it is much safer for adults to consciously communicate with children about relationships and sexuality in a developmentally appropriate way.

What next?

We think you now have enough tools to make a start with relationships and sexuality education whenever you feel ready. Often, after a training session, we find that participants want to start immediately, and when they go home or go to work and try using some of the tools or exercises we have mentioned in our book, they are surprised at how easy they find it! They often tell us that their child or the children they work with were really willing to respond and sometimes even asked them lots more questions. Among many of the comments we have received, one parent of a six-year-old son shared with us: 'After talking about being in love and where babies come from with my child, I not only felt relieved that it wasn't at all difficult, but more than this I felt a much deeper bond with my child. He kissed me afterwards and said, "Can we have another conversation like that tomorrow? I like to talk about these things with you."'

And what rewards can you expect in the longer term from investing your time in learning more about children's relation-ships and sexuality education? For professionals, our previous work suggests that the tips you have picked up from this book should make your role as a sexuality educator slightly easier and, we hope, more fulfilling. For parents and carers, we believe that investing time in sexuality communication with your chil-dren from a young age will mean that the years ahead are less turbulent. Your investment will make it easier for them to com-municate with you, their friends and later with their boyfriends, girlfriends or partners. As one of our children said to us: 'Being used to having lots of conversations about relationships and sexuality at home meant that I grew up feeling so comfortable with this topic. Even more than some of my teachers at school! It gave me confidence to know what I wanted and didn't want, made me more tolerant of others and helped me to be more open minded than some of my friends.'

We wish you all the best in supporting the children in your lives to learn about relationships and sexuality.

With best wishes,
Sanderijn, Clare and Arris

Resources

General

Haffner, D. (2004) *From Diapers to Dating*. New York, NY: Newmarket Press.
Rough, B.J. (2018) *Beyond Birds & Bees*. New York, NY: Seal Press.

Resources about diversity

Gonzales, M.C. (2018) *The Gender Wheel: A Story About Bodies and Gender for Everybody*. San Fransisco: Reflection Press.
Pessin-Whedbee, B. (2016) *Who Are You? The Kids Guide to Gender Identity*. London: Jessica Kingsley Publishers.
Thorn, T. (2019) *It Feels Good to Be Yourself: A Book About Gender Identity*. New York: Henry Holt and Co.
Who Are You? The Kid's Guide to Gender. https://kidsguidetogender.com

Australia

Child Abuse Squad (Western Australia Police) – report child abuse by calling 131 444 or Crime Stoppers 1800 333 000. www.police.wa.gov.au/Your-Safety/Child-Abuse

Child Protection Crisis Care Helpline – (08) 9223 1111 or country free call 1800 199 008. Phone information and counselling service for people in crisis needing urgent help.

Child Protection and Family Support – (08) 9222 2555 or country free call 1800 622 258. Protects and cares for Western Australia children who are in need and supports families and individuals who are at risk or in crisis. www.dcp.wa.gov.au

Child Protection Unit (Perth Children's Hospital) – (08) 6456 4300. 24-hour medical, forensic, social work and therapeutic service for children up to the age of 16 years who may have experienced some form of abuse. www.pch. health.wa.gov.au/our-services/child-protection-unit

eSafety – online safety information. Includes anonymous reporting of offensive and illegal content. www.esafety.gov.au

HealthyWA – information on parenting, immunizations, sexual health, safety and first aid, treatments and healthcare options. www.healthywa.wa.gov.au. This link is for *Talk soon. Talk often. A guide for parents talking to their kids about sex:* www.healthywa.wa.gov.au/Articles/S_T/Talk-soon-talk-often

Kids Helpline – 1800 55 1800. Free confidential 24/7 phone and online counselling service for 5–25-year-olds in Australia. www.kidshelpline.com.au

Ngala Parenting Line – (08) 9368 9368 or 1800 111 546. Free call back phone service (8am to 8pm daily) for support to parents/carers of children up to 18 years. www.ngala.com.au

Parenting WA Line – (08) 6279 1200 or 1800 654 432. 24-hour phone service: information, support and referral service to parents, carers and families with children up to 18 years.

Relationships Australia – 1300 364 277. Relationship support to individuals, families and communities to help achieve positive and respectful relationships. www.relationships.org.au

Safe4Kids – child protection education teaching kids how to identify unsafe situations and seek help for schools and parents. www.safe4kids.com.au

Sex Ed Rescue – a resource for parents. https://sexedrescue.com

Canada

The Access Line – 1 888 642 2725. Confidential 24-hour Canada-wide toll-free number that provides information on reproductive and sexual health.

Action Canada for Sexual Health & Rights – a progressive, pro-choice charitable organization committed to advancing and upholding sexual and reproductive health and rights in Canada and globally. www.actioncanadashr.org

The Canadian Centre for Child Protection – national charity dedicated to the personal safety of all children. Its goal is to reduce the sexual abuse and exploitation of children and prevent child victimization. https://protectchildren.ca/en

Kids Help Phone – 1 800 668 6868. Phone for help for abuse, bullying, cyberbullying, harassment, relationship violence and sexual exploitation or whatever a child wants to talk about. Offers professional counselling, information and referrals for young people in both English and French. https://kidshelpphone.ca

Sex Information & Education Council of Canada (SIECCAN) – *Canadian guidelines for sexual health education* (2019). A guide for educators and policy makers regarding comprehensive sexuality education in Canada. https://siecus.org/wp-content/uploads/2020/03/NSES-2020-2.pdf. SIECCAN is a not-for-profit charitable organization that works with health professionals, educators, community organizations, governments and corporate partners to promote sexual and reproductive health.

SHORE Centre – offers inclusive sexual and reproductive health services that uphold the dignity of everyone. www.shorecentre.ca

UK

Lucy Faithfull Foundation – offers a range of services for individuals and families looking for help, advice, support and intervention with issues relating to child sexual abuse. www.lucyfaithfull.org.uk

Mosac – support, advice and information for non-abusing parents and carers whose children have been sexually abused. www.mosac.org.uk

NSPCC (National Society for the Prevention of Cruelty to Children) – support, advice and information concerning all aspects of children's well-being. www.nspcc.org.uk

Outspoken Sex Ed – a social enterprise which promotes open parent-child sexuality communication. www.outspokeneducation.com

Stop It Now! – confidential freephone helpline for people who are struggling with sexual thoughts and behaviours towards children, or are concerned about someone else's behaviour. www.stopitnow.org.uk

US

Advocates for Youth – focuses on adolescent reproductive and sexual health, strengthening the ability of youth to make informed, responsible decisions about their sexual health. There is also a page for parents on the website as well as a video series to help parents talk to kids from as young as 4 years old to 14 about where babies come from and growing up. https://advocatesforyouth.org

Answer – national organization that provides and promotes unfettered access to comprehensive sexuality education for young people and the adults who teach them. http://answer.rutgers.edu

Child Welfare Information Gateway – promotes the safety, permanency and well-being of children, youth and families by connecting child welfare, adoption and related professionals as well as the public to information, resources and tools covering topics on child welfare, child abuse and neglect, out-of-home care, adoption, and more. www.childwelfare.gov

Committee for Children – provides tools to promote the safety, well-being and success of children in school and in life. www.cfchildren.org

Darkness to Light – empowers adults to prevent, recognize and react responsibly to child sexual abuse through awareness, education and stigma reduction. www.d2l.org

FLASH – sexual health curriculum targeted at children between the ages of five and twelve years and addressing physical development, promotion of sexual health, prevention of disease, interpersonal relationships, body image and gender roles. www.kingcounty.gov/depts/health/locations/family-planning/education.aspx

Lesbian, Gay, Bisexual and Transgender Concerns Office – aims to advance psychology as a means of improving the health and well-being of lesbian, gay, bisexual and transgender people, increasing understanding of gender identity and sexual orientation as aspects of human diversity, and reducing stigma, prejudice, discrimination and violence toward LGBT people. www.apa.org/pi/lgbt

National Center on the Sexual Behavior of Youth (NCSBY) – provides national training and technical assistance to improve the accuracy, accessibility and strategic use of accurate information about the nature, incidence, prevalence, prevention, treatment and management of youth with problematic sexual behaviour. www.ncsby.org

National Sex Education Standards, Second Edition – outlines the foundational knowledge and skills students need to navigate sexual development and grow into sexually healthy adults. https://advocatesforyouth.org/wp-content/uploads/2020/03/NSES-2020-web.pdf

Netsmartz – provides information on internet safety including sexting, social media, gaming, cyberbullying and so on. www.missingkids.org/NetSmartz

Planned Parenthood – delivers information and materials on reproductive health care and sex education to millions of people worldwide, and for parents. www.plannedparenthood.org

Sexuality Information and Education Council of the United States (SIECUS) – asserts that sex education is a powerful vehicle for social change. It views sexuality as a fundamental part of being human, one worthy of dignity and respect. It advocates for the rights of all people to accurate information, comprehensive sexuality education and the full spectrum of sexual and reproductive health services. https://siecus.org

Sexuality Resource Center for Parents – helps parents provide positive comprehensive sexuality education, raising sexually healthy and happy children. http://srcp.org/index.html

Stop It Now! – prevents the sexual abuse of children by mobilizing adults, families and communities to take actions that protect children before they are harmed. www.stopitnow.org

References

Introduction

1. Pound, P., Denford, S., Shucksmith, J., Tanton C. *et al.* (2017) 'What is best practice in sex and relationship education? A synthesis of evidence, including stakeholders' views.' *BMJ Open 7*, 5, e014791.
2. Montgomery, P. and Knerr, W. (2018) *Review of the evidence on sexuality education: Report to inform the update of the UNESCO International Technical Guidance on Sexuality Education.* Paris: UNESCO.

Chapter 1

1. Graaf, H. (2010) *Parenting and Adolescents' Sexual Health.* Utrecht: Eburon.
2. Baumrind, D. (1971) 'Current patterns of parental authority.' *Developmental Psychology 4*, 1 Pt.2, 1–103.
3. Graaf, H., Vanwesenbeeck, I., Woertman, L., Keijsers, L., Meijer, S. and Meeus, W. (2010) 'Parental support and knowledge and adolescents' sexual health: Testing two mediational models in a national Dutch sample.' *Journal of Youth and Adolescence 39*, 2, 189–198.
4. Graaf, H., Vanwesenbeeck, I., Woertman, L. and Meeus, W. (2011) 'Parenting and adolescents' sexual development in western societies: A literature review.' *European Psychologist 16*, 1, 21–31.
5. Gottman, J. and DeClaire, J. (1997) *The Heart of Parenting: How to Raise an Emotionally Intelligent Child.* New York, NY: Simon & Schuster.

6. Goleman, D. (1995) *Emotional Intelligence: Why It Can Matter More Than IQ.* New York, NY: Bantam.
7. UNICEF UK (2011) *Children's Well-Being in UK, Sweden and Spain.* Available at: www.ipsos.com/ipsos-mori/en-uk/childrens-well-being-uk-sweden-and-spain
8. UNICEF UK (2013) *The Well-Being of Children: Short Version of the Report for Young People in the UK.* Available at: www.unicef.org.uk/publications/report-card-11-child-wellbeing-what-do-you-think
9. Rees, G. and Bradshaw, J. (2016) 'Exploring low subjective well-being among children aged 11 in the UK: An analysis using data reported by parents and by children.' *Child Indicators Research, 11*, 1, 27–56. https://doi.org/10.1007/s12187-016-9421-z
10. Rademakers, J., Laan, M. and Straver, C. (2003) 'Body Awareness and Physical Intimacy: An Exploratory Study.' In J. Bancroft (ed.) *Sexual Development in Childhood.* Bloomington, IN: Indiana University Press.
11. Graaf, H., van den Borne, M., Nikkelen, S., Twisk, D. and Meijer, S. (2017) *Seks onder je 25e (Sex Under the Age of 25).* Utrecht: Rutgers/Soa Aids, Eburon. Available at: https://seksonderje25e.nl/english
12. Rothman, E.F., Paruk, J., Espensen, A., Temple, J.R. and Adams, K. (2017) 'A qualitative study of what US parents say and do when their young children see pornography.' *Academic Pediatrics 17*, 8, 844–849.
13. BBFC (2019) *Research into Children and Pornography.* Available at: www.bbfc.co.uk/about-us/news/children-see-pornography-as-young-as-seven-new-report-finds
14. Townsend, C. and Rheingold, A.A. (2013) *Estimating a Child Sexual Abuse Prevalence Rate for Practitioners: A Review of Child Sexual Abuse Prevalence Studies.* Charleston, SC: Darkness to Light.
15. Rape Abuse and Incest National Network (RAINN) (2020) *Child Sexual Abuse Statistics.* Available at: www.rainn.org/articles/child-sexual-abuse

Chapter 2

1. International Planned Parenthood Federation (IPPF) (2010) *IPPF Framework for Comprehensive Sexuality Education.* London: IPPF.
2. Rademakers, J., Laan, M. and Straver, C. (2003) 'Body Awareness and Physical Intimacy: An Exploratory Study.' In J. Bancroft (ed.) *Sexual Development in Childhood.* Bloomington, IN: Indiana University Press.
3. Reynolds, M.A., Herbenick, D.L. and Bancroft, J.H. (2003) 'The Nature of Childhood Sexual Experiences: Two Studies 50 Years Apart.' In J. Bancroft

(ed.) *Sexual Development in Childhood*. Bloomington, IN: Indiana University Press.

4. Montgomery, P. and Knerr, W. (2018) *Review of the evidence on sexuality education: Report to inform the update of the UNESCO International Technical Guidance on Sexuality Education*. Paris: UNESCO.

5. AgeChecked (2019) *Over Half of UK Children Use Social Media Before Reaching Secondary School*. Available at: www.telemediaonline.co.uk/over-half-of-uk-children-use-social-media-before-reaching-secondary-school

Chapter 3

1. Palama, A., Malsert, J. and Gentaz, E. (2018) 'Are 6-month-old human infants able to transfer emotional information (happy or angry) from voices to faces? An eye-tracking study.' *PLoS ONE, 13*, 4, e0194579 doi: 10.1371/journal.pone.0194579

2. Byers, E.S., Sears, H.A. and Weaver, A.D. (2008) 'Parents' reports of sexual communication with children in kindergarten to grade 8.' *Journal of Marriage and Family, 70*, 1, 86–96.

3. Graaf, H., van den Borne, M., Nikkelen, S., Twisk, D. and Meijer, S. (2017) *Seks onder je 25ᵉ (Sex Under the Age of 25)*. Utrecht: Rutgers/Soa Aids, Eburon.

4. Graaf, H. (2013) 'Bloemetjes en bijtjes of zaadjes en eitjes? (Opvattingen over) seksuele opvoeding in Nederland.' *Pedagogiek 33*, 1, 21–36.

5. Bos, H.M.W, Lisette, K. and Gartrell, N.K. (2018) 'A population-based comparison of female and male same-sex parent and different-sex parent households.' *Family Process, 57*, 1: 148–164.

Chapter 4

1. Slaughter, V., Peterson, C. and Mackintosh, E. (2007) 'Mind what mother says: Narrative input and theory of mind in typical children and those on the autism spectrum.' *Child Development, 78*, 3, 839–858.

2. Ruffman, T., Slade, L. and Crowe, E. (2003) 'The relation between children's and mothers' mental state language and theory-of-mind understanding.' *Child Development, 73*, 3, 734–751.

3. Sussman, F. (2006) *TalkAbility™ – People skills for verbal children on the autism spectrum: A guide for parents*. Toronto: Hanen Early Language Program.

4. Goleman, D. (1995) *Emotional Intelligence: Why It Can Matter More Than IQ*. New York, NY: Bantam.

5. Goleman, D. (2007) *Social Intelligence: The New Science of Human Relationships.* London: Arrow Books.
6. Condry, J. and Condry, S. (1976) 'Sex differences: A study of the eye of the beholder.' *Child Development, 47*, 3, 812–819.
7. Donovan, W., Taylor, N. and Leavitt, L. (2007) 'Maternal sensory sensitivity and response bias in detecting change in infant facial expressions: Maternal self-efficacy and infant gender labelling.' *Infant Behavior and Development, 30*, 3, 436–452.
8. Kuebli, J. and Fivush, R. (1992) 'Gender differences in parent-child conversations about past emotions.' *Sex Roles: A Journal of Research, 27*, 11–12, 683–698.
9. Condry, S.M, Condry, J.C. and Pogatshnik, L.W. (1983) 'Sex differences: A study of the ear of the beholder.' *Sex Roles, 9*, 6, 697–704.
10. Rough, B.J. (2018) *Beyond Birds and Bees: Bringing Home a New Message to Our Kids about Sex, Love and Equality.* New York, NY: Seal Press.
11. Kohlberg, L. (1966) 'A Cognitive-Developmental Analysis of Children's Sex-Role Concepts and Attitudes.' In E. Maccoby (ed.) *The Development of Sex Differences.* London: Tavistock.

Chapter 5

1. World Health Organization Regional Office for Europe and BZgA (2010) *Standards for Sexuality Education in Europe.* BZgA Cologne: Federal Centre for Health Education. Available at: www.bzga-whocc.de/fileadmin/user_upload/WHO_BZgA_Standards_English.pdf
2. UNESCO (2018) *International Technical Guidance on Sexuality Education: An Evidence-Informed Approach.* Paris: UNESCO. Available at: https://unesdoc.unesco.org/ark:/48223/pf0000260770
3. Sexuality Information and Education Council of the United States (2004) *Guidelines for Comprehensive Sexuality Education* (third edition). New York, NY: SIECUS. Available at: https://siecus.org/resources/the-guidelines
4. Western Australian Department of Health (2019) *Talk soon. Talk often. A guide for parents talking to their kids about sex.* State of Western Australia: Department of Health. Available at: www.healthywa.wa.gov.au/Articles/S_T/Talk-soon-Talk-often
5. Unicef (n.d.) *Skin-To-Skin Contact.* Available at: https://www.unicef.org.uk/babyfriendly/baby-friendly-resources/implementing-standards-resources/skin-to-skin-contact

6. K. Shutts et al. (2017) 'Early Preschool Environments and Gender: Effects of Gender Pedagogy in Sweden.' *Journal of Experimental Child Psychology, 162*, 1–17.

Chapter 6

1. Laura K. Murray *et al.* (2014) 'Child Sexual Abuse.' *Child and Adolescent Psychiatric Clinics of North America., 23*, 2, 321–337.
2. K. Murayama *et al.* (2016) 'Don't aim too high for your kids.' *Journal of Personality and Social Psychology 111*, 5, 766–779.
3. Krauss, S., Orth, U. and Robins, R.W. (2020) 'Family environment and self-esteem development: A longitudinal study from age 10 to 16.' *Journal of Personality and Social Psychology, 119*, 2, 457–478.
4. Brummelman, E., Thomaes, S., Overbeek, G., Orobio de Castro, B., van den Hout, M.A. and Bushman, B.J. (2014) 'On feeding those hungry for praise: Person praise backfires in children with low self-esteem.' *Journal of Experimental Psychology: General, 143*, 1, 9–14. doi:10.1037/a0031917
5. Kellogg, N.D. (2010) 'Sexual behaviors in children: Evaluation and management.' *American Family Physician, 82*, 10, 1233–1238.
6. Janssen, D.F. (2007) 'Cultural notes on orgasm, ejaculation, and wet dreams.' *The Journal of Sex Research, 44*, 2, 122–134.

Chapter 7

1. Bleidorn, W., Arslan, R.C., Denissen, J.J., Rentfrow, P.J. *et al.* (2016) 'Age and gender differences in self-esteem: A cross-cultural window.' *Journal of Personality and Social Psychology, 111*, 3, 396–410.
2. Fine, C. (2010) *Delusions of Gender: How Our Minds, Society, and Neurosexism Create Difference.* New York, NY: W.W. Norton.
3. Harris, J.R. (1998) *The Nurture Assumption: Why Children Turn Out the Way They Do.* New York, NY: The Free Press.
4. Bos, H.M.W., Lisette, K. and Gartrell, N.K. (2018) 'A population-based comparison of female and male same-sex parent and different-sex parent households.' *Family Process, 57*, 1, 148–164.
5. Rademakers, J., Laan, M. and Straver, C. (2003) 'Body awareness and physical intimacy: An exploratory study.' In J. Bancroft (ed.) *Sexual Development in Childhood.* Bloomington: Indiana University Press.

6. Institute of Medicine (US) Committee on Lesbian, Gay, Bisexual, and Transgender Health Issues and Research Gaps and Opportunities (2011) *The Health of Lesbian, Gay, Bisexual, and Transgender People: Building a Foundation for Better Understanding.* Washington (DC): National Academies Press.

Chapter 8

1. Mandal, A. (2018) Health guide for young women regarding labiaplasty. Available at: www.news-medical.net/news/20180313/Health-guide-for-young-women-regarding-labiaplasty.aspx
2. Van Lunsen, R. and Laan, E. (2017) *Seks!* Amsterdam: Prometheus.
3. Stubbs, M. (2008) 'Cultural perceptions and practices around menarche and adolescent menstruation in the United States.' *Annals of the New York Academy of Sciences, 1135*, 1, 58–66.
4. Graaf, H., van den Borne, M., Nikkelen, S., Twisk, D. and Meijer, S. (2017) *Seks onder je 25e (Sex Under the Age of 25).* Utrecht: Rutgers/Soa Aids, Eburon. Available at: https://seksonderje25e.nl/english
5. Graaf, H., Kruijer, H., van Acker, J. and Meijer, S. (2012) *Seks onder je 25e (Sex Under the Age of 25).* Utrecht: Rutgers/Soa Aids, Eburon. Available at: www.rutgers.international/sites/rutgersorg/files/PDF/Summary_Sexunderageof25_ENG.pdf
6. Rademakers, J., Laan, M. and Straver, C. (2003) Body awareness and physical intimacy: An exploratory study. In J. Bancroft (ed) *Sexual Development in Childhood.* Bloomington: Indiana University Press.
7. Bos, H. (2017) 'Roze gezinnen' ('Pink Families') *De pedagoog, 04*, 18, December.
8. Institute of Medicine (US) Committee on Lesbian, Gay, Bisexual, and Transgender Health Issues and Research Gaps and Opportunities (2011) *The Health of Lesbian, Gay, Bisexual, and Transgender People: Building a Foundation for Better Understanding.* Washington (DC): National Academies Press.

Chapter 9

1. Frans, E. (2018) *Sensoa Flag System, Reacting to sexually (un)acceptable behaviour of children and young people.* Antwerpen/Apeldoorn: Sensoa/Garant. Available at: https://shop.rutgers.nl/en/shop/themes/sexual-education/the-sensoa-flag-system-%C2%A9/197683&page=

.